UNBURDENED

THE ART OF RELEASING THE PAST

DR. MINAKSHI BANSAL

Contents

Contents

Prayer

"Om Bhadram Karnebhih Shrinuyama Devah

Bhadram Pashyemakshabhiryajatrah

Sthirairangais Tushtuvamsastanubhih

Vyashema Devahitam Yadayuh

Svasti Na Indro Vriddhashravah

Svasti Nah Pusha Vishwavedah

Svasti Nastarkshyo Arishtanemih

Svasti No Brihaspatir Dadhatu

Om Shantih Shantih Shantih"

This mantra is a prayer for universal well-being, invoking the blessings of various deities for protection, health, and happiness. It emphasizes the importance of experiencing the auspicious through all senses and living a life aligned with divine purpose. The repetition of "Shantih" at the end signifies a deep desire for peace in the individual, the environment, and the universe at large. This mantra is often recited as a prayer for peace, prosperity, and the physical and spiritual well-being of all beings.

🌿🌿🌿

About The Author

This book represents the culmination of extensive research and meticulous analysis, incorporating a diverse range of sources, including numerous books, scholarly studies, and personal experiences. Additionally, I have scoured various websites to gather relevant information and data essential for the compilation of this work. I have taken every precaution to ensure the accuracy of the information presented and have diligently cited all sources to acknowledge their contributions.

From her earliest days, Minakshi was distinguished by an insatiable appetite for reading. Her literary universe was inhabited by characters and narratives that spanned ethical tales, motivational and inspirational stories, and the mythic parables imbued with life lessons. This voracious reading habit was not merely for personal edification but was driven by a desire to distill and disseminate the essence of these narratives to foster the development of students and peers alike. She was particularly captivated by the lives and teachings of historical figures and spiritual leaders such as Adi Shankaracharya, Swami Vivekananda, Dr. APJ Abdul Kalam, Mahamana Pandit Madan Mohan Malviya, Mahatma Gandhi, Sardar Vallabhai Patel, and Vinoba Bhave, among others. Their philosophies and life stories fueled her ambition to embody their ideals of resilience, selflessness, and relentless pursuit of knowledge.

Dr. Minakshi's academic and practical engagement with psychology has been equally noteworthy. As a research scholar, her focus has been on exploring the intricate tapestry of the human psyche, aiming to unlock the potential for psychological well-being and societal harmony. Her scholarly work is complemented by her active involvement in social work, where she employs her academic insights to make tangible differences in the lives of the underprivileged. Her endeavours in social work are characterized by an innovative approach that combines traditional wisdom with contemporary psychological practices to address the multifaceted challenges faced by these communities.

Her artistic talents, another facet of her diverse capabilities, are not merely a personal passion but also serve as a medium through which she communicates and connects with others. Her art, rich in symbolism and emotional depth, reflects her philosophical inquiries and social concerns, offering viewers a glimpse into the breadth of her intellect and the depth of her compassion.

In addition to her contributions to the arts and social sciences, Dr. Minakshi has embraced the healing arts of Pranic Healing, mastering the techniques developed by Master Choa Kok Sui. This practice, which focuses on the manipulation of Prana or life energy to heal the body and aura, has been both a personal journey of discovery and a means through which she extends her healing touch to others. Her proficiency in Pranic Healing is complemented by her advocacy and teaching of various forms of meditation aimed at rejuvenation, personal betterment, and the cultivation of harmony within individuals and communities alike.

Dr. Minakshi's life is a narrative of relentless pursuit, not just of personal achievement but of the upliftment and empowerment of society at large. Her diverse interests and talents—spanning the arts, literature, psychology, and the healing practices—converge on a singular path of service. She embodies the spirit of the luminaries who inspired her, channelling their legacy through her actions and teachings. Through her books, art, and social initiatives, she continues to inspire a new generation to embark on their own journeys of self-discovery, resilience, and altruism.

Her commitment to social betterment, particularly her focus on uplifting underprivileged children, reflects a deep understanding of the transformative potential of education and personal development. By integrating her knowledge of psychology, her artistic sensibilities, and her healing practices, Dr. Bansal has developed a holistic approach to social work that addresses both the immediate needs and the long-term well-being of the communities she serves.

As an author, Dr. Minakshi's writings offer a blend of inspirational insights, practical wisdom, and reflective contemplations drawn from her extensive reading and life experiences. Her books serve as a guide for those seeking to navigate the complexities of life with grace, resilience, and purpose. Through her narratives, she extends an invitation to her readers to explore the depths of their own potential and to contribute meaningfully to the collective well-being of society.

In Dr. Minakshi Bansal, we find a remarkable synthesis of the artist, the scholar, the healer, and the social activist. Her life's work stands as a beacon of hope and a source of inspiration for individuals seeking to make a difference in the world. Her story is a compelling reminder of the power of individual action, rooted in compassion and driven by a profound commitment to the betterment of humanity. Dr. Minakshi's legacy is not just in the tangible outcomes of her efforts but in the enduring spirit of inquiry, empathy, and service that she embodies.

ppp

Preface

As I sit down to write the preface to this book, I am reminded of the countless conversations, reflections, and moments of introspection that have brought me to this point. This book is a culmination of my personal journey, professional experiences, and deep-seated passion for understanding the human condition. It is born out of a desire to help others navigate the often tumultuous waters of their past, to find healing, and to embrace a future unburdened by the weight of what has come before.

Throughout my life, I have been both a witness and participant in the profound struggle to release the past. It is a universal challenge that transcends cultures, backgrounds, and life experiences. We all carry with us the echoes of our histories—our triumphs and traumas, our joys and sorrows. These experiences shape us, often in ways we do not fully comprehend, and they can either anchor us in a state of pain or propel us toward growth and liberation. This book is an exploration of that journey from pain to peace, from being weighed down by the past to becoming unburdened and free.

In my own life, I have faced moments where the past seemed insurmountable, where regrets and unresolved emotions threatened to overshadow the present. I have experienced the deep sense of loss that accompanies missed opportunities and the lingering sting of past mistakes. Yet, it is through these very experiences that I have discovered the incredible resilience of the human spirit. I have learned that healing is not a linear process but a dynamic, ever-evolving journey. It requires courage, compassion, and a willingness to face the shadows of our past with an open heart.

One of the most powerful lessons I have learned is the importance of acknowledging and embracing our stories. Each of us has a unique narrative, woven from the threads of our experiences, relationships, and inner struggles. It is through understanding and honoring these stories that we can begin to release their hold on us. This book is an invitation to delve deeply into your own story, to uncover the hidden wounds that may still be influencing your life, and to find the strength to rewrite your narrative in a way that empowers and uplifts you.

Forgiveness is a central theme in this journey of releasing the past. It is a concept that is often misunderstood and fraught with complexity. Forgiveness is not about condoning the actions that have caused us harm, nor is it about forgetting the pain we have endured. Rather, it is a conscious decision to release the grip of anger and resentment, to free ourselves from the chains of bitterness that bind us to our past. Forgiveness is a gift we give ourselves, a path to inner peace and freedom. It is through forgiveness that we can transform our wounds into sources of strength and compassion.

Another critical aspect of this journey is the practice of mindfulness. Mindfulness is the art of being fully present in the moment, of observing our thoughts and emotions without judgment. It allows us to become aware of the ways in which the past may be influencing our present, and it gives us the tools to respond to our experiences with greater clarity and intentionality. Through mindfulness, we can cultivate a deeper sense of self-awareness and develop the capacity to release the patterns of thought and behavior that no longer serve us.

As I wrote this book, I was continually reminded of the incredible power of community and support. Healing is not a solitary endeavor; it is a journey that is enriched and deepened by the presence of others who walk alongside us. Whether through the support of friends, family, or professional guides, we are reminded that we do not have to navigate this path alone. Connection and compassion from others can provide the encouragement and strength we need to face our past and move forward with hope and resilience.

Throughout the pages of this book, you will find a blend of personal reflections, practical exercises, and insights drawn from both ancient wisdom and contemporary psychology. My hope is that these elements will offer you a comprehensive and holistic approach to releasing the past. Each chapter is designed to guide you through different aspects of this journey, from understanding the weight of your past to embracing change, letting go of guilt, and ultimately rewriting your story in a way that reflects your true self.

The process of writing this book has been both a labor of love and a deeply transformative experience for me. It has required me to confront my own past, to examine my own wounds and to find the courage to share my journey with you. In doing so, I have come to realize that we are all connected by our shared humanity, by our collective struggles and triumphs. It is my sincere hope that my words will resonate with you, that they will provide you with the guidance and inspiration you need to embark on your own journey of healing and transformation.

As you read this book, I encourage you to approach it with an open heart and a willingness to explore the depths of your own experiences. Take the time to reflect on the exercises and to engage with the questions and prompts provided. Allow yourself the space to feel, to process, and to heal. Remember that this journey is uniquely yours, and there is no right or wrong way to navigate it. Trust in your own inner wisdom and know that you have the strength and resilience to overcome whatever challenges you may face.

In closing, I want to express my deepest gratitude to you, the reader. Your willingness to embark on this journey of self-discovery and healing is a testament to your courage and your commitment to living a more authentic and fulfilling life. It is my honor to walk alongside you on this path, to offer you the insights and tools that have been so transformative in my own life. May this book serve as a beacon of hope and a source of strength as you move forward, unburdened by the past and empowered to embrace the future with open arms.

Dr. Minakshi Bansal
Social Activist
Ahmedabad, Gujarat, Bharat

❦❦❦

ONE

Introduction: The Weight of the Past

The past is a powerful force in our lives, shaping our experiences, emotions, and identities in profound ways. It can be a source of joy and nostalgia, bringing memories of happy times and achievements that we cherish. However, it can also be a heavy burden, filled with regrets, mistakes, traumas, and unresolved emotions that weigh us down and hinder our ability to live fully in the present. The weight of the past can manifest in various forms, such as recurring negative thoughts, persistent feelings of guilt or shame, and patterns of behavior that keep us stuck in unproductive cycles. Understanding and addressing this burden is essential for personal growth and emotional well-being.

The influence of the past begins in childhood, where early experiences and relationships lay the foundation for our understanding of the world and ourselves. Positive experiences can instill a sense of security and confidence, while negative ones can leave lasting scars. These early memories often become ingrained in our subconscious, influencing our thoughts, feelings, and actions in ways we may not fully realize. As we grow older, additional layers of experiences are added, each contributing to the complex tapestry of our personal history.

One of the most significant ways the past can burden us is through the presence of unresolved emotions. Painful experiences, such as the loss of a loved one, a traumatic event, or a significant failure, can leave deep emotional wounds. If these wounds are not properly addressed and healed, they can fester and continue to affect us long after the events themselves have passed. Unresolved emotions can lead to a range of psychological issues, including anxiety, depression, and chronic stress. They can also impact our relationships, causing us to react defensively or withdraw from those we care about.

Another way the past can weigh us down is through the lingering effects of regret. Regret is a powerful emotion that arises when we feel that we have made a wrong decision or missed an important opportunity. It is often accompanied by a sense of loss and a longing to go back and change what happened. While it is natural to experience some regret, dwelling on it can be detrimental to our mental health. Constantly ruminating on past mistakes can erode our self-esteem and prevent us from taking positive steps forward.

Guilt is another heavy burden that can arise from the past. It is the feeling of responsibility for a wrongdoing or a failure to act. Guilt can be constructive when it motivates us to make amends and improve our behavior. However, when it becomes overwhelming or irrational, it can be paralyzing. Excessive guilt can lead to feelings of worthlessness and self-loathing, making it difficult to move on from past transgressions.

Trauma is perhaps the most profound way the past can affect us. Traumatic experiences, such as abuse, violence, or accidents, can have a lasting impact on our mental and physical health. Trauma can disrupt our sense of safety and trust, leading to symptoms such as flashbacks, hypervigilance, and emotional numbness. The effects of trauma can be pervasive, affecting every aspect of our lives and making it challenging to engage with the present.

The weight of the past is not just an individual experience; it can also be a collective one. Historical events, such as wars, social injustices, and cultural upheavals, can leave a legacy of trauma and unresolved issues that are passed down through generations. This collective burden can influence our identities and relationships, shaping the way we view ourselves and others. It can also create a sense of shared suffering and a need for collective healing and reconciliation.

Despite the significant impact the past can have on our lives, it is important to recognize that we are not powerless in the face of it. While we cannot change what has happened, we can change how we respond to it and how we allow it to influence our present and future. This process begins with acknowledgment and acceptance. Acknowledging the past means facing it honestly and without denial. It involves recognizing the events and experiences that have shaped us, as well as the emotions and beliefs that arise from them. Acceptance, on the other hand, means embracing the reality of the past without judgment. It is about letting go of the need to change what cannot be changed and finding peace with what has been.

Forgiveness is a powerful tool in the process of releasing the past. Forgiveness is often misunderstood as condoning or excusing wrongdoing, but it is actually about freeing ourselves from the emotional hold of the past. It is a conscious decision to let go of resentment and anger, allowing us to move forward with a lighter heart. Forgiveness can be directed towards others who have hurt us, as well as towards ourselves for our own mistakes and shortcomings. It is a process that takes time and effort, but it can lead to profound healing and liberation.

Another important aspect of releasing the past is the practice of mindfulness. Mindfulness involves paying attention to the present moment with curiosity and non-judgment. It allows us to observe our thoughts and emotions without getting caught up in them. By cultivating mindfulness, we can develop a greater awareness of how the past influences our current experiences and learn to respond to it in a more intentional and compassionate way. Mindfulness practices, such as meditation and deep breathing, can help us stay grounded in the present and reduce the power of past memories over our lives.

Rewriting our personal narratives is another effective strategy for releasing the past. Our memories are not static; they are shaped by the stories we tell ourselves about them. By changing the way we interpret and frame our past experiences, we can transform their impact on our lives. This process involves identifying and challenging negative or limiting beliefs that have arisen from past events and replacing them with more empowering and positive perspectives. It is about finding meaning and growth in our experiences, even in the midst of pain and difficulty.

Seeking closure is also a key component of letting go of the past. Closure involves finding a sense of resolution and completeness with past events. It can come from various sources, such as having a meaningful conversation, performing a ritual, or creating a symbolic act of letting go. Closure is not always possible in every situation, but finding ways to create a sense of finality can help us move forward with greater clarity and peace.

Creating healthy boundaries is essential for protecting our emotional well-being and preventing the past from intruding on our present. Boundaries are the limits we set for ourselves in our interactions with others and our environment. They help us define what is acceptable and what is not, allowing us to take control of our own experiences. Establishing boundaries can involve distancing ourselves from toxic relationships, setting limits on our time and energy, and creating spaces for self-care and reflection.

Practicing self-compassion is crucial for healing and releasing the past. Self-compassion involves treating ourselves with kindness and understanding, especially in moments of pain and struggle. It means recognizing our own humanity and the fact that we all make mistakes and face challenges. By cultivating self-compassion, we can reduce feelings of guilt and shame and foster a more supportive and nurturing relationship with ourselves.

Support from others is often invaluable in the process of letting go of the past. Friends, family, and professionals can provide empathy, guidance, and encouragement as we navigate our healing journey. Sharing our experiences and emotions with trusted individuals can help us feel less isolated and more understood. Therapy and counseling can offer additional tools and techniques for addressing unresolved issues and developing healthier coping mechanisms.

Transforming negative patterns that have arisen from the past is essential for creating a more positive and fulfilling present. Negative patterns can include habitual thoughts, behaviors, and reactions that are rooted in past experiences. Identifying these patterns requires self-awareness and reflection, as well as a willingness to change. By consciously choosing new ways of thinking and acting, we can break free from unproductive cycles and create new, healthier habits.

Cultivating gratitude is a powerful practice for shifting our focus from the burdens of the past to the blessings of the present. Gratitude involves recognizing and appreciating the positive aspects of our lives, no matter how small. It helps us develop a more optimistic and resilient mindset, allowing us to find joy and meaning even in the midst of challenges. Keeping a gratitude journal, expressing thanks to others, and savoring positive moments are all ways to foster a sense of gratitude.

Living authentically means embracing our true selves and aligning our actions with our values and beliefs. It involves letting go of the need to conform to others' expectations and finding the courage to be genuine and vulnerable. Living authentically requires self-awareness and a commitment to personal integrity. It allows us to create a life that is true to who we are and free from the constraints of past conditioning.

The journey of self-discovery is an ongoing process of exploring and understanding our inner selves. It involves delving into our thoughts, emotions, and motivations, as well as our strengths and weaknesses. Self-discovery helps us gain insight into the ways the past has shaped us and empowers us to make conscious choices about our future. Practices such as journaling, meditation, and introspection can facilitate this journey and lead to greater self-awareness and self-acceptance.

Moving forward with purpose means setting intentions and goals that reflect our true desires and aspirations. It involves creating a vision for our future that is based on our values and passions, rather than being dictated by past experiences. By focusing on our purpose and taking deliberate steps towards it, we can create a more fulfilling and meaningful life. Purpose gives us direction and motivation, helping us navigate challenges and setbacks with resilience and determination.

In conclusion, the weight of the past can be a significant burden, but it is not insurmountable. By acknowledging and accepting our past, practicing forgiveness and mindfulness, rewriting our narratives, seeking closure, creating healthy boundaries, and cultivating self-compassion and gratitude, we can release the hold of past experiences and move forward with greater freedom and joy. The journey of letting go is not always easy, but it is a path to healing and liberation that allows us to live more fully in the present and embrace the possibilities of the future.

❦❦❦

"Healing begins with acknowledging the shadows of our past. It is through understanding and embracing our stories that we find the strength to rewrite them. In this acceptance, we uncover the power to move forward."

TWO

ACKNOWLEDGING YOUR PAST

Acknowledging the past is a crucial step in the journey of self-discovery and personal growth. It involves a conscious and deliberate effort to recognize and accept the events, experiences, and emotions that have shaped our lives. This process can be challenging and uncomfortable, as it often requires us to confront painful memories and unresolved feelings. However, by acknowledging our past, we can begin to understand how it influences our present behavior and thoughts, and take steps toward healing and moving forward.

One of the fundamental aspects of acknowledging the past is the act of facing our memories. Our minds have a natural tendency to avoid or suppress painful experiences, a defense mechanism that can temporarily shield us from emotional distress. While this can be beneficial in the short term, it often leads to unresolved issues that continue to affect us subconsciously. By bringing these memories into conscious awareness, we can begin to process and understand them. This does not mean reliving the pain or getting stuck in it, but rather observing and accepting it as part of our history.

Memory is a complex and often unreliable construct. Our

recollections of past events are influenced by our emotions, perceptions, and the passage of time. Acknowledging the past involves recognizing that our memories may not be entirely accurate or complete, but they are still valid and significant. It is important to approach our past with curiosity and openness, rather than judgment or denial. This allows us to see the broader context of our experiences and understand how they have contributed to our development.

Emotional honesty is a key component of acknowledging the past. This means being truthful with ourselves about how past events have affected us emotionally. It requires us to identify and name our feelings, whether they are sadness, anger, fear, guilt, or shame. These emotions are often complex and intertwined, and it can take time to unravel them. By acknowledging our true feelings, we can begin to address and heal the emotional wounds that have been left behind.

Another important aspect of acknowledging the past is understanding the impact of our early experiences and relationships. Our childhood and formative years play a significant role in shaping our personalities, beliefs, and behaviors. Positive experiences, such as love, support, and encouragement, can foster a sense of security and self-worth. Conversely, negative experiences, such as neglect, abuse, or trauma, can leave deep emotional scars and influence our patterns of thinking and relating to others. Recognizing the influence of these early experiences can help us make sense of our current behaviors and challenges.

Acknowledging the past also involves taking responsibility for our actions and decisions. It is natural to feel defensive or to blame others for our difficulties, but true growth comes from owning our part in our life story. This does not mean taking on undue guilt or blame, but rather accepting that we have the power to shape our lives moving forward. By acknowledging our role in past events, we can learn from our mistakes and make more conscious choices in the future.

Forgiveness is an essential part of acknowledging the past. This includes forgiving others who have hurt us, as well as forgiving ourselves for our own mistakes and shortcomings. Forgiveness is not about condoning or excusing harmful behavior, but rather about releasing the hold that resentment and anger have on us. It is a process of letting go that allows us to move forward with a lighter heart. Forgiveness can be difficult, especially when the wounds are deep, but it is a necessary step toward healing and liberation.

Mindfulness is a powerful tool in the process of acknowledging the past. By practicing mindfulness, we can develop greater awareness of our thoughts and emotions as they arise. This allows us to observe our reactions to past memories without getting overwhelmed by them. Mindfulness helps us stay grounded in the present moment, reducing the power of past experiences to dictate our current state of mind. Techniques such as meditation, deep breathing, and mindful movement can help us cultivate this awareness and create a sense of inner calm.

Rewriting our personal narratives is another important strategy for acknowledging and integrating our past. Our memories are shaped by the stories we tell ourselves about them. These narratives can be limiting or empowering, depending on how we frame them. By consciously choosing to reframe our experiences in a more positive and constructive light, we can transform their impact on our lives. This involves identifying negative or limiting beliefs that have arisen from past events and replacing them with more empowering and affirming perspectives. It is about finding meaning and growth in our experiences, even in the midst of pain and difficulty.

Seeking closure is a vital part of acknowledging the past. Closure involves finding a sense of resolution and completeness with past events. This can come from various sources, such as having a meaningful conversation, performing a ritual, or creating a symbolic act of letting go. Closure is not always possible in every situation, but finding ways to create a sense of finality can help us move forward with greater clarity and peace. It allows us to release the emotional hold of the past and make space for new experiences and opportunities.

Creating healthy boundaries is essential for protecting our emotional well-being and preventing the past from intruding on our present. Boundaries are the limits we set for ourselves in our interactions with others and our environment. They help us define what is acceptable and what is not, allowing us to take control of our own experiences. Establishing boundaries can involve distancing ourselves from toxic relationships, setting limits on our time and energy, and creating spaces for self-care and reflection. By creating and maintaining healthy boundaries, we can protect ourselves from being overwhelmed by past experiences and focus on our present and future well-being.

Self-compassion is crucial for healing and acknowledging the past. Self-compassion involves treating ourselves with kindness and understanding, especially in moments of pain and struggle. It means recognizing our own humanity and the fact that we all make mistakes and face challenges. By cultivating self-compassion, we can reduce feelings of guilt and shame and foster a more supportive and nurturing relationship with ourselves. Self-compassion allows us to approach our past with gentleness and empathy, rather than harsh judgment or criticism.

Support from others is often invaluable in the process of acknowledging the past. Friends, family, and professionals can provide empathy, guidance, and encouragement as we navigate our healing journey. Sharing our experiences and emotions with trusted individuals can help us feel less isolated and more understood.

Therapy and counseling can offer additional tools and techniques for addressing unresolved issues and developing healthier coping mechanisms. Support groups and community resources can also provide a sense of connection and validation as we work through our past.

Transforming negative patterns that have arisen from the past is essential for creating a more positive and fulfilling present. Negative patterns can include habitual thoughts, behaviors, and reactions that are rooted in past experiences. Identifying these patterns requires self-awareness and reflection, as well as a willingness to change. By consciously choosing new ways of thinking and acting, we can break free from unproductive cycles and create new, healthier habits. This transformation is a gradual process that requires patience and persistence, but it can lead to profound personal growth and empowerment.

Cultivating gratitude is a powerful practice for shifting our focus from the burdens of the past to the blessings of the present. Gratitude involves recognizing and appreciating the positive aspects of our lives, no matter how small. It helps us develop a more optimistic and resilient mindset, allowing us to find joy and meaning even in the midst of challenges. Keeping a gratitude journal, expressing thanks to others, and savoring positive moments are all ways to foster a sense of gratitude. By focusing on what we are grateful for, we can reduce the emotional hold of past negative experiences and cultivate a greater sense of well-being.

Living authentically means embracing our true selves and aligning our actions with our values and beliefs. It involves letting go of the need to conform to others' expectations and finding the courage to be genuine and vulnerable. Living authentically requires self-awareness and a commitment to personal integrity. It allows us to create a life that is true to who we are and free from the constraints of past conditioning. By living authentically, we can honor our past experiences while also creating a more meaningful and fulfilling present and future.

The journey of self-discovery is an ongoing process of exploring and understanding our inner selves. It involves delving into our thoughts, emotions, and motivations, as well as our strengths and weaknesses. Self-discovery helps us gain insight into the ways the past has shaped us and empowers us to make conscious choices about our future. Practices such as journaling, meditation, and introspection can facilitate this journey and lead to greater self-awareness and self-acceptance. Self-discovery is not about finding definitive answers, but rather about continually learning and growing as individuals.

Moving forward with purpose means setting intentions and goals that reflect our true desires and aspirations. It involves creating a vision for our future that is based on our values and passions, rather than being dictated by past experiences. By focusing on our purpose and taking deliberate steps towards it, we can create a more fulfilling and meaningful life. Purpose gives us direction and motivation, helping us navigate challenges and setbacks with resilience and determination. It allows us to move beyond the limitations of our past and embrace the possibilities of our future.

Acknowledging the past is not about dwelling on it or becoming defined by it. Rather, it is about integrating our experiences into our sense of self in a way that allows us to grow and thrive. It is about recognizing the impact of the past while also understanding that we have the power to shape our present and future. By acknowledging our past, we can release its emotional hold, heal our wounds, and create a life that is aligned with our true selves. The journey of acknowledging the past is a courageous and transformative one, leading to greater self-awareness, healing, and personal growth.

ϷϷϷ

"Forgiveness is not about excusing the past but freeing ourselves from its chains. It is an act of self-liberation, allowing us to transform pain into peace. Through forgiveness, we find the path to inner freedom."

THREE

THE POWER OF FORGIVENESS

Forgiveness is one of the most powerful and transformative acts we can undertake in our lives. It is often misunderstood as a passive or weak response to wrongdoing, but in reality, forgiveness requires immense strength, courage, and compassion. It is a conscious decision to let go of resentment, anger, and the desire for revenge, and to instead cultivate empathy, understanding, and peace. The power of forgiveness lies in its ability to heal emotional wounds, restore relationships, and free us from the burdens of the past.

At its core, forgiveness is about releasing the hold that negative emotions have on us. When we are hurt or wronged by someone, it is natural to feel anger, betrayal, and resentment. These emotions are valid and serve as important signals that our boundaries have been violated. However, holding on to these feelings for an extended period can be detrimental to our well-being. Resentment and anger can consume our thoughts and energy, leading to chronic stress, anxiety, and even physical health issues. They can also prevent us from moving forward and experiencing joy and fulfillment in our lives. Forgiveness allows us to let go of these toxic emotions and create space for healing and growth.

Forgiveness is not about condoning or excusing harmful behavior. It does not mean that we accept or approve of the actions that caused us pain. Rather, it is about acknowledging the reality of what happened and choosing to respond in a way that promotes our own well-being. Forgiveness involves a shift in perspective, from focusing on the harm that was done to us to understanding the broader context of the situation. This shift can help us see the person who hurt us as a flawed human being, rather than as a villain or enemy. It allows us to recognize that everyone makes mistakes and that we all have the capacity for both good and bad actions.

Empathy is a crucial component of forgiveness. Empathy involves putting ourselves in the shoes of the other person and trying to understand their thoughts, feelings, and motivations. This does not mean that we have to agree with or justify their behavior, but it can help us see the situation from a different angle. Often, people who hurt others are themselves dealing with their own pain, insecurities, and struggles. By cultivating empathy, we can develop a more compassionate and nuanced understanding of their actions. This understanding can help us soften our anger and open the door to forgiveness.

Forgiveness is also an act of self-compassion. When we forgive, we are not only releasing the other person from the burden of our resentment, but we are also freeing ourselves from the grip of negative emotions. Holding on to anger and resentment can create a cycle of suffering, where we continuously relive the pain and keep ourselves stuck in a state of hurt. Forgiveness breaks this cycle and allows us to move forward with a lighter heart. It is a gift we give to ourselves, a way of reclaiming our peace and well-being.

The process of forgiveness can be challenging and often takes time. It is not a one-time event, but rather a journey that involves multiple stages. The first step is to acknowledge the hurt and the impact it has had on us. This requires us to be honest with ourselves about our feelings and to allow ourselves to fully experience the pain. It is important to validate our emotions and to understand that it is okay to feel hurt and angry.

The next step is to make a conscious decision to forgive. This decision is often the most difficult part, as it involves letting go of our desire for revenge or retribution. It requires us to prioritize our own healing and well-being over the need to punish the other person. This does not mean that we have to forget what happened or that we have to reconcile with the person who hurt us. Forgiveness can be a private and internal process, where we release the negative emotions within ourselves without necessarily involving the other person.

Once we have made the decision to forgive, the next step is to work on cultivating empathy and understanding. This can involve reflecting on the other person's background, experiences, and challenges, and considering what might have led them to act in the way they did. It can also involve seeking to understand the broader context of the situation and recognizing that we all have moments of weakness and imperfection. This step requires an open and compassionate mindset, as well as a willingness to see beyond our own pain.

As we work on cultivating empathy, it is also important to focus on our own healing. This can involve engaging in practices that promote emotional and physical well-being, such as therapy, meditation, exercise, and self-care. It can also involve seeking support from friends, family, or support groups, where we can share our experiences and receive encouragement and understanding. Healing is a gradual process, and it is important to be patient and gentle with ourselves as we navigate this journey.

Forgiveness is not always easy, and there may be times when we struggle to let go of our anger and resentment. It is important to acknowledge and honor these feelings, rather than suppressing or denying them. We can allow ourselves to feel the full range of our emotions while also holding on to the intention to forgive. This intention can serve as a guiding light, helping us stay focused on our goal of healing and peace, even when the path is difficult.

Forgiveness can have profound benefits for our mental and physical health. Research has shown that forgiving others can lead to reduced stress, lower blood pressure, and improved immune function. It can also lead to greater emotional well-being, including increased happiness, reduced anxiety, and a greater sense of connection and empathy. By letting go of negative emotions, we create space for positive emotions and experiences to flourish.

Forgiveness can also have a transformative impact on our relationships. When we forgive, we open the door to reconciliation and healing. This does not mean that we have to rebuild the relationship in the same way it was before, but it can create an opportunity for a new and healthier dynamic. Forgiveness can lead to greater understanding, trust, and communication, and it can help us build stronger and more resilient connections with others.

In addition to forgiving others, it is also important to practice self-forgiveness. We are often our own harshest critics, and we can carry a heavy burden of guilt and self-blame for our own mistakes and shortcomings. Self-forgiveness involves recognizing that we are human and that we all make mistakes. It requires us to treat ourselves with the same compassion and understanding that we would offer to a friend. By forgiving ourselves, we can release the weight of our own guilt and shame and move forward with greater self-acceptance and self-love.

Self-forgiveness is a process that involves several steps. The first step is to acknowledge and take responsibility for our actions. This requires us to be honest with ourselves about our mistakes and to recognize the impact they may have had on others. It is important to differentiate between taking responsibility and taking on undue guilt or blame. We can own our actions without letting them define our entire sense of self-worth.

The next step is to make amends and take corrective action where possible. This can involve apologizing to those we have hurt, making reparations, and committing to change our behavior in the future. Making amends can help us feel a sense of closure and can contribute to the healing process for both ourselves and others.

Once we have taken responsibility and made amends, the next step is to practice self-compassion. This involves treating ourselves with kindness and understanding, recognizing that we are doing our best and that we are deserving of forgiveness. Self-compassion can be cultivated through practices such as mindfulness, self-reflection, and affirmations. It can also involve seeking support from others who can offer us empathy and encouragement.

The final step in self-forgiveness is to let go of self-judgment and to embrace a sense of renewal. This involves releasing the hold that guilt and shame have on us and allowing ourselves to move forward with a fresh perspective. It requires us to trust in our own capacity for growth and change and to believe in our own worthiness of forgiveness and love.

The power of forgiveness extends beyond the individual to the collective level. Societies and communities that embrace forgiveness can create a culture of empathy, understanding, and reconciliation. This can lead to greater social cohesion, reduced conflict, and a more just and compassionate world. Collective forgiveness involves addressing historical and systemic injustices, acknowledging the harm that has been done, and working towards healing and restoration. It requires a commitment to truth, accountability, and empathy, and it can lead to profound social transformation.

In conclusion, forgiveness is a powerful and transformative act that has the potential to heal emotional wounds, restore relationships, and free us from the burdens of the past. It requires strength, courage, and compassion, and it involves a process of acknowledging our hurt, making a conscious decision to forgive, cultivating empathy, and focusing on our own healing. Forgiveness is not about condoning harmful behavior, but about releasing the hold that negative emotions have on us and creating space for peace and well-being. It can have profound benefits for our mental and physical health, and it can lead to stronger and more resilient relationships. Self-forgiveness is also essential, as it allows us to release guilt and shame and to move forward with greater self-acceptance and self-love. The power of forgiveness extends to the collective level, where it can contribute to social cohesion and justice. By embracing forgiveness, we can create a more compassionate and just world, and we can experience the profound healing and liberation that comes from letting go of resentment and embracing empathy and understanding.

"Mindfulness is the art of being fully present, allowing us to observe our thoughts and emotions without judgment. It grants us the clarity to see how the past influences the present. With mindfulness, we cultivate the power to choose our responses."

FOUR

EMBRACING CHANGE

Embracing change is an essential aspect of personal growth and development. Change is a constant in life, whether we seek it out or it happens unexpectedly. It can be challenging, as it often involves stepping out of our comfort zones and facing the unknown. However, embracing change can lead to significant opportunities for learning, growth, and transformation. By cultivating a positive attitude towards change and developing strategies to navigate it effectively, we can harness its potential and create a more fulfilling and resilient life.

Change comes in many forms. It can be external, such as a new job, a move to a different city, the end of a relationship, or global events that impact our lives. It can also be internal, such as shifts in our beliefs, values, or goals. Regardless of its nature, change often triggers a range of emotions, including fear, anxiety, excitement, and hope. These emotions are natural responses to the uncertainty and disruption that change brings. Understanding and acknowledging these feelings is the first step in embracing change.

One of the primary reasons change is difficult is because it disrupts our routines and habits. Human beings are creatures of habit; we find comfort and security in familiar patterns and predictable environments. When these are altered, it can create a sense of instability and loss of control. However, it is important to recognize that while change can be uncomfortable, it is also a catalyst for growth. It challenges us to adapt, learn new skills, and develop resilience. Embracing change means shifting our perspective from seeing it as a threat to viewing it as an opportunity.

A positive mindset is crucial in the process of embracing change. This involves cultivating an attitude of openness, curiosity, and optimism. Instead of focusing on what we might lose or the difficulties we might face, we can choose to focus on the possibilities and potential benefits that change can bring. This shift in perspective can help us approach change with a sense of adventure and excitement, rather than fear and resistance. It is about seeing change as a natural part of life and an opportunity for personal and professional development.

Developing flexibility and adaptability is another key aspect of embracing change. Flexibility allows us to adjust our plans and expectations in response to new circumstances. It involves being willing to let go of rigid ideas and approaches and to explore alternative solutions. Adaptability, on the other hand, is about our capacity to adjust to new conditions and thrive in different environments. Both qualities are essential in navigating change effectively. They enable us to respond proactively and creatively to challenges, rather than feeling overwhelmed or defeated.

One effective strategy for embracing change is to break it down into manageable steps. Large or sudden changes can feel overwhelming, but by dividing them into smaller, actionable tasks, we can make the process more manageable and less intimidating. This approach allows us to focus on one step at a time, reducing the sense of being overwhelmed and increasing our sense of control. It also provides a clear path forward, helping us to stay motivated and engaged as we navigate the change.

Another important strategy is to seek support from others. Change can be a lonely experience, but it does not have to be faced alone. Friends, family, colleagues, and mentors can provide valuable support, encouragement, and perspective. Sharing our experiences and feelings with trusted individuals can help us feel understood and less isolated. They can also offer practical advice and insights that we might not have considered. Additionally, professional support, such as coaching or therapy, can provide guidance and tools to help us navigate change more effectively.

Self-care is essential during times of change. Change can be stressful, and it is important to take care of our physical, emotional, and mental well-being. This includes getting enough rest, eating healthily, exercising regularly, and engaging in activities that bring us joy and relaxation. Self-care also involves setting boundaries and giving ourselves permission to take breaks and recharge. By prioritizing self-care, we can build the resilience and energy needed to navigate change successfully.

Mindfulness is a powerful tool for embracing change. Mindfulness involves paying attention to the present moment with curiosity and non-judgment. It helps us become more aware of our thoughts, emotions, and reactions, allowing us to respond to change with greater clarity and calm. Mindfulness practices, such as meditation, deep breathing, and mindful movement, can help reduce stress and increase our ability to stay grounded during times of change. They also enhance our capacity for self-reflection, helping us to gain insights into our patterns and responses.

Embracing change also involves setting goals and intentions. Having a clear sense of direction and purpose can help us stay focused and motivated as we navigate change. Goals provide us with a sense of purpose and direction, while intentions help us stay aligned with our values and priorities. Setting realistic and achievable goals allows us to measure our progress and celebrate our successes along the way. It also helps us stay proactive and engaged, rather than feeling passive or reactive in the face of change.

Another important aspect of embracing change is developing a growth mindset. A growth mindset is the belief that our abilities and intelligence can be developed through effort, learning, and perseverance. This mindset encourages us to see challenges as opportunities for growth and to view failures as valuable learning experiences. By adopting a growth mindset, we can approach change with greater confidence and resilience, knowing that we have the capacity to learn and adapt.

Resilience is a critical quality for embracing change. Resilience is the ability to bounce back from adversity and to remain strong and flexible in the face of challenges. It involves developing coping strategies and a positive outlook that allows us to navigate difficulties with grace and determination. Resilience can be built through practices such as gratitude, positive self-talk, and connecting with our support network. By cultivating resilience, we can better withstand the stresses and uncertainties of change and emerge stronger and more empowered.

Reflection is an essential part of the process of embracing change. Taking the time to reflect on our experiences and to consider what we have learned can provide valuable insights and growth. Reflection allows us to identify patterns, recognize our strengths and weaknesses, and understand the impact of our actions and decisions. It also helps us to integrate new experiences into our sense of self and to develop a deeper understanding of our goals and values. Journaling, meditation, and conversations with trusted individuals can all be valuable tools for reflection.

Embracing change also involves letting go of the past. Holding on to old ways of thinking and being can prevent us from fully engaging with new opportunities and experiences. Letting go does not mean forgetting or dismissing the past, but rather accepting it and allowing ourselves to move forward. It involves releasing the need for things to stay the same and being open to new possibilities. Letting go can be a challenging process, but it is essential for growth and transformation.

One of the most powerful aspects of embracing change is the opportunity for personal transformation. Change challenges us to re-evaluate our beliefs, behaviors, and goals, and to make adjustments that align with our true selves. It allows us to shed old patterns and to develop new, more fulfilling ways of being. Personal transformation is a continuous process that involves self-discovery, growth, and the pursuit of our highest potential. By embracing change, we can unlock new levels of self-awareness, creativity, and fulfillment.

In addition to personal transformation, embracing change can also lead to positive impacts on our relationships and communities. Change can inspire us to connect with others in new ways, to collaborate and to support each other through transitions. It can also encourage us to contribute to the greater good and to make a positive difference in the world. By embracing change with an open heart and a positive attitude, we can inspire and uplift those around us and create a ripple effect of growth and transformation.

Ultimately, embracing change is about cultivating a sense of trust and faith in ourselves and in the process of life. It involves believing in our own capacity to navigate challenges and to create a meaningful and fulfilling life. It also involves trusting that change is a natural and necessary part of growth, and that it can lead to new and exciting opportunities. By developing this sense of trust and faith, we can approach change with greater confidence and ease, knowing that we have the strength and resilience to handle whatever comes our way.

In conclusion, embracing change is a powerful and transformative process that can lead to significant personal and professional growth. It involves cultivating a positive attitude, developing flexibility and adaptability, seeking support, prioritizing self-care, practicing mindfulness, setting goals, and developing a growth mindset. It also involves letting go of the past, reflecting on our experiences, and embracing the opportunity for personal transformation. By approaching change with openness, curiosity, and trust, we can navigate the uncertainties of life with greater resilience and fulfillment. Embracing change allows us to unlock our full potential and to create a life that is aligned with our true selves and our highest aspirations.

"Our stories are unique tapestries woven from our experiences, relationships, and inner struggles. By honoring these narratives, we release their hold on us. This respect for our journey fuels our personal growth."

FIVE

LETTING GO OF GUILT

Letting go of guilt is a profound and liberating process that is essential for emotional well-being and personal growth. Guilt is a powerful emotion that arises when we believe we have done something wrong or failed to meet our own or others' expectations. While guilt can sometimes serve a constructive purpose by motivating us to make amends and improve our behavior, excessive or prolonged guilt can be debilitating. It can lead to feelings of worthlessness, depression, and anxiety, and it can prevent us from fully enjoying life and moving forward. Understanding the nature of guilt and developing strategies to release it can help us lead healthier, more fulfilling lives.

Guilt often stems from a sense of responsibility and a desire to adhere to moral or ethical standards. It can arise from specific actions, such as hurting someone or failing to fulfill a commitment, or from broader issues, such as feeling inadequate in our roles as parents, partners, or professionals. Guilt can also be triggered by internalized societal or cultural expectations, which may impose unrealistic standards of behavior and success. Regardless of its source, guilt is often accompanied by self-criticism and a harsh judgment of oneself. This self-judgment can create a cycle of negative thinking that reinforces feelings of guilt and prevents us from finding peace.

The first step in letting go of guilt is to acknowledge and understand it. This involves recognizing the specific thoughts and beliefs that are causing the guilt and examining their validity. It is important to differentiate between rational and irrational guilt. Rational guilt arises when we have genuinely done something wrong and need to take responsibility for our actions. Irrational guilt, on the other hand, is based on unrealistic or exaggerated perceptions of wrongdoing. By identifying whether our guilt is rational or irrational, we can begin to address it more effectively.

For rational guilt, taking responsibility and making amends is crucial. This may involve apologizing to those we have hurt, making reparations, or taking steps to change our behavior. Taking responsibility allows us to acknowledge our mistakes and demonstrate a commitment to personal growth and improvement. It can also help to alleviate feelings of guilt by showing that we are willing to take corrective action. However, it is important to remember that making amends is not about seeking forgiveness from others, but rather about doing what we believe is right and just.

In cases of irrational guilt, it is important to challenge and reframe the negative thoughts and beliefs that are causing the guilt. This involves questioning the validity of these thoughts and considering alternative, more balanced perspectives. For example, we might ask ourselves whether we are holding ourselves to an unrealistic standard or whether we are taking on more responsibility than is fair or reasonable. Cognitive-behavioral techniques, such as identifying cognitive distortions and replacing them with more rational thoughts, can be helpful in this process. By challenging irrational guilt, we can begin to release the undue burden it places on us.

Self-compassion is a key component of letting go of guilt. Self-compassion involves treating ourselves with the same kindness and understanding that we would offer to a friend. It means recognizing that we are human and that making mistakes is a natural part of life. Instead of berating ourselves for our shortcomings, we can choose to respond with empathy and support. Self-compassion can help to counteract the harsh self-criticism that often accompanies guilt and can create a more nurturing and forgiving inner dialogue.

Mindfulness is another powerful tool for releasing guilt. Mindfulness involves paying attention to the present moment with curiosity and non-judgment. It helps us become more aware of our thoughts and emotions, allowing us to observe them without becoming overwhelmed or entangled. By practicing mindfulness, we can develop greater awareness of the guilt we are experiencing and create space to respond to it more skillfully. Mindfulness practices, such as meditation, deep breathing, and mindful movement, can help to reduce the intensity of guilt and create a sense of inner calm.

Forgiveness is an essential aspect of letting go of guilt. This includes both forgiving ourselves for our mistakes and, when appropriate, seeking forgiveness from others. Self-forgiveness involves acknowledging our imperfections and accepting that we are worthy of love and compassion, despite our flaws. It means letting go of the need for self-punishment and allowing ourselves to move forward with a sense of renewal. Seeking forgiveness from others can also be a healing process, as it allows us to express remorse and make amends. However, it is important to recognize that forgiveness from others is not always possible, and our healing should not be contingent on their response.

Another important aspect of letting go of guilt is setting healthy boundaries. Boundaries help us to define our responsibilities and to avoid taking on more than we can reasonably handle. They allow us to protect our emotional well-being and to prioritize our own needs and values. Setting boundaries can involve saying no to unreasonable demands, delegating tasks, and seeking support when needed. By establishing and maintaining healthy boundaries, we can prevent the accumulation of guilt that arises from overextending ourselves or trying to meet unrealistic expectations.

Reflection and self-awareness are crucial for understanding the deeper roots of our guilt. This involves exploring the underlying beliefs, values, and experiences that contribute to our feelings of guilt. Journaling, therapy, and introspective practices can provide valuable insights into the sources of our guilt and help us to develop a more nuanced understanding of ourselves. Reflection allows us to identify patterns and triggers, and to develop strategies for addressing them more effectively. It also helps us to gain clarity about our values and to align our actions with our true priorities.

Gratitude is a powerful practice for shifting our focus from guilt to appreciation. By cultivating gratitude, we can redirect our attention to the positive aspects of our lives and the things we are thankful for. This practice helps to create a more balanced perspective and can counteract the negative impact of guilt. Keeping a gratitude journal, expressing thanks to others, and savoring positive moments are all ways to incorporate gratitude into our daily lives. By focusing on what we are grateful for, we can reduce the emotional hold of guilt and create a greater sense of well-being.

Developing a growth mindset is another important strategy for letting go of guilt. A growth mindset is the belief that our abilities and intelligence can be developed through effort, learning, and perseverance. This mindset encourages us to see mistakes and challenges as opportunities for growth and learning, rather than as failures. By adopting a growth mindset, we can approach our mistakes with curiosity and a willingness to learn, rather than with self-judgment and guilt. This shift in perspective allows us to embrace our imperfections and to see them as part of our journey toward personal and professional development.

Support from others is invaluable in the process of letting go of guilt. Friends, family, and professionals can provide empathy, encouragement, and perspective. Sharing our experiences and feelings with trusted individuals can help us feel understood and less isolated. They can also offer practical advice and insights that we might not have considered. Therapy and counseling can provide additional tools and techniques for addressing guilt and developing healthier coping mechanisms. Support groups and community resources can also provide a sense of connection and validation as we work through our guilt.

Letting go of guilt is not a linear process; it involves ongoing effort and practice. There may be times when feelings of guilt resurface, and it is important to approach these moments with patience and self-compassion. It is natural to experience setbacks and to struggle with letting go, but each step forward, no matter how small, contributes to our overall healing and growth. By consistently practicing the strategies outlined above, we can gradually release the hold of guilt and create a more positive and empowering relationship with ourselves.

In conclusion, letting go of guilt is a transformative and liberating process that is essential for emotional well-being and personal growth. It involves acknowledging and understanding the nature of our guilt, taking responsibility for our actions, challenging irrational guilt, and practicing self-compassion and mindfulness. Forgiveness, both of ourselves and others, is a key aspect of releasing guilt, as is setting healthy boundaries and engaging in reflection and self-awareness. Cultivating gratitude, developing a growth mindset, and seeking support from others are also important strategies for letting go of guilt. By embracing these practices, we can free ourselves from the burden of guilt and create a more fulfilling and resilient life. Letting go of guilt allows us to move forward with a greater sense of peace, self-acceptance, and empowerment, and to fully engage with the present and future.

❧❧❧

"Resilience is born from the courage to face our wounds and the compassion to heal them. It is the strength to rise above our past and create a future filled with hope. With resilience, we transform challenges into opportunities."

SIX
OVERCOMING REGRET

Overcoming regret is a profound and often challenging journey that involves understanding, processing, and ultimately letting go of the past to embrace the present and future with a renewed sense of purpose and hope. Regret is a complex emotion that arises when we reflect on past actions, decisions, or missed opportunities and feel sorrow or disappointment over what might have been. It can be a paralyzing emotion, trapping us in a cycle of rumination and preventing us from moving forward. However, by addressing and overcoming regret, we can transform our relationship with the past and cultivate a more fulfilling and resilient life.

Regret often stems from a sense of loss or missed potential. We may regret things we did, such as saying hurtful words or making poor decisions, or things we did not do, such as failing to pursue a dream or not taking a chance on a relationship or opportunity. These regrets can weigh heavily on us, as they represent moments where we feel we fell short of our ideals or missed out on what could have been. This sense of loss can be compounded by feelings of guilt, shame, and self-blame, which can further intensify our regret and make it difficult to move on.

The first step in overcoming regret is to acknowledge and accept it. This involves recognizing the specific actions or decisions that we regret and allowing ourselves to fully experience the associated emotions. It is important to approach this process with compassion and non-judgment, understanding that regret is a natural part of the human experience. Everyone makes mistakes and encounters missed opportunities, and feeling regret is a sign that we care about our actions and their impact. By acknowledging our regret, we can begin to understand its sources and start the process of healing.

Reflection and self-awareness are crucial in understanding the root causes of our regret. This involves examining the circumstances and motivations behind our actions and decisions, as well as the values and expectations that influenced them. Reflecting on our past can provide valuable insights into our patterns of behavior and thinking, helping us to identify any underlying issues or beliefs that may have contributed to our regret. It can also help us to gain a clearer perspective on what we have learned from these experiences and how they have shaped who we are today.

Self-compassion is essential in the process of overcoming regret. This means treating ourselves with kindness and understanding, rather than harsh criticism and self-blame. It involves recognizing that we are human and that making mistakes is a natural part of life. By practicing self-compassion, we can create a more supportive and nurturing inner dialogue, which can help to alleviate the pain of regret and promote healing. Self-compassion also allows us to acknowledge our efforts and intentions, even if the outcomes were not as we had hoped.

Forgiveness is a powerful tool for overcoming regret. This includes both forgiving ourselves for our mistakes and, if applicable, forgiving others who may have been involved. Self-forgiveness involves letting go of the need for self-punishment and accepting that we did the best we could with the knowledge and resources we had at the time. It means recognizing that we are worthy of love and compassion, despite our imperfections. Forgiving others can also be an important part of the healing process, as it allows us to release any lingering resentment or anger that may be contributing to our regret.

Reframing our perspective on regret can also be helpful. Instead of viewing regret as a negative and paralyzing force, we can choose to see it as an opportunity for growth and learning. This involves shifting our focus from what we lost or missed out on to what we gained from the experience. Every regret carries with it valuable lessons that can inform our future actions and decisions. By identifying and embracing these lessons, we can transform our regret into a source of wisdom and resilience.

Setting goals and intentions for the future is another important strategy for overcoming regret. This involves using the insights and lessons we have gained from our past experiences to inform our future choices and actions. By setting clear and achievable goals, we can create a sense of direction and purpose that can help to alleviate the feelings of stagnation and helplessness that often accompany regret. It also allows us to focus our energy on positive and constructive endeavors, rather than dwelling on the past.

Taking action is a crucial part of the process of overcoming regret. This can involve making amends, if possible, for any harm we may have caused, or taking steps to pursue opportunities or goals that we previously missed. Taking action can help to restore a sense of agency and control, which can be empowering and healing. It also demonstrates our commitment to growth and change, reinforcing our belief in our ability to create a positive future.

Mindfulness is a valuable practice for managing and overcoming regret. Mindfulness involves paying attention to the present moment with curiosity and non-judgment. It helps us to become more aware of our thoughts and emotions, allowing us to observe them without becoming overwhelmed or entangled. By practicing mindfulness, we can develop a greater sense of acceptance and equanimity, which can help to reduce the intensity of our regret and create a sense of inner peace. Mindfulness practices, such as meditation, deep breathing, and mindful movement, can also help to ground us in the present moment and cultivate a sense of calm and clarity.

Gratitude is another powerful practice for overcoming regret. By cultivating gratitude, we can shift our focus from what we have lost or missed out on to what we have and what we appreciate in our lives. This practice can help to create a more balanced and positive perspective, counteracting the negative impact of regret. Keeping a gratitude journal, expressing thanks to others, and savoring positive moments are all ways to incorporate gratitude into our daily lives. By focusing on what we are grateful for, we can create a greater sense of well-being and contentment.

Building and maintaining a support network is also important in the process of overcoming regret. Friends, family, and professionals can provide empathy, encouragement, and perspective. Sharing our experiences and feelings with trusted individuals can help us feel understood and less isolated. They can also offer practical advice and insights that we might not have considered. Therapy and counseling can provide additional tools and techniques for addressing regret and developing healthier coping mechanisms. Support groups and community resources can also provide a sense of connection and validation as we work through our regret.

Resilience is a critical quality for overcoming regret. Resilience is the ability to bounce back from adversity and to remain strong and flexible in the face of challenges. It involves developing coping strategies and a positive outlook that allows us to navigate difficulties with grace and determination. Resilience can be built through practices such as gratitude, positive self-talk, and connecting with our support network. By cultivating resilience, we can better withstand the stresses and uncertainties of life and emerge stronger and more empowered.

It is important to recognize that overcoming regret is not a linear process. It involves ongoing effort and practice, and there may be times when feelings of regret resurface. It is important to approach these moments with patience and self-compassion, understanding that healing is a gradual and continuous journey. By consistently practicing the strategies outlined above, we can gradually release the hold of regret and create a more positive and empowering relationship with ourselves.

Letting go of regret also involves embracing the present moment and the opportunities it offers. This means focusing on what we can do now to create a fulfilling and meaningful life, rather than dwelling on what might have been. It involves making the most of our current circumstances and being open to new possibilities. By living in the present and embracing the opportunities it offers, we can create a more vibrant and joyful life.

In conclusion, overcoming regret is a transformative and empowering process that involves understanding, processing, and ultimately letting go of the past. It involves acknowledging and accepting our regret, reflecting on its root causes, and practicing self-compassion and forgiveness. Reframing our perspective on regret, setting goals and intentions for the future, taking action, and practicing mindfulness and gratitude are all important strategies for overcoming regret. Building and maintaining a support network, developing resilience, and embracing the present moment are also crucial components of this process. By embracing these practices, we can free ourselves from the burden of regret and create a more fulfilling and resilient life. Overcoming regret allows us to move forward with a greater sense of peace, self-acceptance, and empowerment, and to fully engage with the present and future.

❧❧❧

"Living authentically means aligning our actions with our true selves. It is the courage to express our deepest values and passions. Through authenticity, we build a life of integrity and fulfillment."

SEVEN
HEALING EMOTIONAL WOUNDS

Healing emotional wounds is a deeply personal and often challenging journey that requires time, patience, and self-compassion. Emotional wounds can result from a variety of experiences, including loss, trauma, betrayal, or any event that leaves a lasting impact on our hearts and minds. These wounds can affect our ability to trust, feel joy, and connect with others, and they can manifest in various forms, such as anxiety, depression, or chronic stress. Healing these wounds is essential for our overall well-being and personal growth, as it allows us to move forward with a renewed sense of peace and wholeness.

The first step in healing emotional wounds is acknowledging their presence. Many people try to suppress or ignore their pain, hoping it will fade away over time. However, unaddressed emotional wounds can fester and grow, impacting various aspects of our lives. Recognizing and accepting that we are hurt is crucial. It involves giving ourselves permission to feel the pain without judgment. This acknowledgment can be the hardest part, as it requires us to face our vulnerabilities and confront the sources of our distress.

Once we acknowledge our emotional wounds, the next step is to explore their origins. Understanding where our pain comes from can provide valuable insights into how it affects us. This process often involves reflecting on past experiences and identifying the events or relationships that contributed to our suffering. Journaling can be a useful tool for this reflection, as it allows us to express our thoughts and feelings freely. Writing about our experiences can help us make sense of them and uncover patterns that we may not have noticed before.

Seeking professional help can be an important part of the healing process. Therapists and counselors are trained to help individuals navigate their emotional pain and develop strategies for coping and healing. Therapy provides a safe and supportive environment to explore our feelings, gain new perspectives, and learn effective coping mechanisms. Different therapeutic approaches, such as cognitive-behavioral therapy, psychodynamic therapy, or trauma-focused therapy, can be tailored to our specific needs and experiences.

In addition to professional help, building a strong support system is essential for healing. Friends, family, and loved ones can offer emotional support, understanding, and companionship during difficult times. Sharing our experiences with trusted individuals can help us feel less isolated and more connected. It is important to communicate our needs and boundaries to our support system, as they may not always know how to help unless we express our feelings and preferences clearly.

Practicing self-compassion is a vital aspect of healing emotional wounds. Self-compassion involves treating ourselves with kindness and understanding, especially during times of pain and difficulty. It means recognizing that suffering is a part of the human experience and that we are not alone in our struggles. By being gentle with ourselves, we can reduce self-criticism and create a nurturing environment for healing. Self-compassion can be cultivated through mindfulness practices, positive self-talk, and self-care activities that bring us comfort and joy.

Mindfulness is another powerful tool for healing emotional wounds. Mindfulness involves paying attention to the present moment with curiosity and non-judgment. It helps us become more aware of our thoughts, emotions, and bodily sensations, allowing us to observe them without becoming overwhelmed. Mindfulness practices, such as meditation, deep breathing, and yoga, can help us stay grounded and centered. These practices can reduce stress, increase emotional resilience, and create a sense of inner calm that supports the healing process.

Forgiveness is often a critical component of healing emotional wounds. This includes both forgiving others who have hurt us and forgiving ourselves for any perceived mistakes or shortcomings. Forgiveness does not mean condoning harmful behavior, but rather releasing the hold that anger and resentment have on us. It is a process of letting go that allows us to move forward with a lighter heart. Self-forgiveness involves recognizing that we are human and that making mistakes is a natural part of life. By practicing forgiveness, we can free ourselves from the burden of past grievances and create space for healing and growth.

Engaging in creative activities can also be a therapeutic way to heal emotional wounds. Art, music, writing, and other forms of creative expression allow us to process and release our emotions in a non-verbal and intuitive way. These activities can provide a sense of accomplishment and joy, helping to shift our focus from pain to creativity and self-expression. Creativity can be a powerful outlet for healing, as it allows us to explore our inner world and communicate our feelings in a unique and personal way.

Physical activity is another important aspect of the healing process. Exercise has been shown to have numerous benefits for mental health, including reducing symptoms of depression and anxiety, improving mood, and increasing overall well-being. Physical activity can help release built-up tension and stress, and it can also provide a sense of routine and purpose. Whether it's walking, running, dancing, or practicing yoga, finding a form of exercise that we enjoy can support our emotional healing.

Establishing healthy boundaries is crucial for protecting our emotional well-being. Boundaries help us define what is acceptable and what is not in our relationships and interactions with others. They allow us to protect our energy and prioritize our needs. Setting boundaries can involve saying no to requests that feel overwhelming, limiting contact with individuals who drain our energy, and creating time for self-care and relaxation. By establishing and maintaining healthy boundaries, we can create a safe and supportive environment for healing.

Developing resilience is essential for navigating the challenges of emotional healing. Resilience is the ability to bounce back from adversity and to adapt to difficult circumstances. It involves cultivating a positive outlook, developing effective coping strategies, and maintaining a sense of hope and determination. Resilience can be built through practices such as gratitude, positive self-talk, and connecting with supportive individuals. By developing resilience, we can better withstand the ups and downs of the healing process and emerge stronger and more empowered.

Spirituality can also play a significant role in healing emotional wounds. For many people, spirituality provides a sense of meaning, purpose, and connection to something greater than themselves. Whether through religious practices, meditation, or a connection to nature, spirituality can offer comfort and solace during times of pain. It can also provide a framework for understanding our experiences and finding a sense of peace and acceptance. Exploring our spiritual beliefs and practices can support our emotional healing and provide a source of strength and inspiration.

It is important to recognize that healing emotional wounds is a gradual and ongoing process. There may be times when we feel stuck or overwhelmed, and it is important to approach these moments with patience and self-compassion. Healing is not a linear journey; it involves progress, setbacks, and moments of reflection and growth. By consistently practicing the strategies outlined above, we can gradually release the hold of our emotional wounds and create a more positive and empowering relationship with ourselves.

Celebrating small victories and milestones is an important part of the healing process. Acknowledging our progress, no matter how small, can provide motivation and encouragement. It reminds us that healing is possible and that we are capable of overcoming our challenges. Celebrating our achievements can also help to shift our focus from pain to growth and resilience. Whether through journaling, sharing our successes with others, or treating ourselves to something special, taking the time to celebrate our progress can reinforce our commitment to healing.

Ultimately, healing emotional wounds is about creating a sense of wholeness and integration within ourselves. It involves bringing together the various parts of our experiences, both positive and negative, and finding a way to move forward with a sense of peace and acceptance. It is about honoring our pain and our resilience, and recognizing that we are more than our wounds. By embracing the healing process with courage and compassion, we can transform our relationship with our past and create a brighter and more fulfilling future.

In conclusion, healing emotional wounds is a deeply personal and transformative journey that requires time, patience, and self-compassion. It involves acknowledging and understanding our pain, seeking professional help and support, practicing self-compassion and mindfulness, and engaging in creative and physical activities. Setting healthy boundaries, developing resilience, and exploring spirituality can also support the healing process. By consistently practicing these strategies, we can gradually release the hold of our emotional wounds and create a more positive and empowering relationship with ourselves. Healing emotional wounds allows us to move forward with a greater sense of peace, self-acceptance, and empowerment, and to fully engage with the present and future.

"Embracing change is an essential part of growth. It requires letting go of the familiar and stepping into the unknown. In this willingness to change, we find the potential for new beginnings."

EIGHT

THE ROLE OF MINDFULNESS

Mindfulness plays a vital role in our overall well-being and personal development. At its core, mindfulness is the practice of paying attention to the present moment with an attitude of openness, curiosity, and non-judgment. This seemingly simple concept can have profound effects on our mental, emotional, and physical health. By cultivating mindfulness, we can enhance our ability to cope with stress, improve our relationships, and foster a deeper understanding of ourselves and the world around us. The practice of mindfulness can be integrated into various aspects of our lives, helping us to navigate the complexities of modern living with greater ease and resilience.

One of the fundamental aspects of mindfulness is its emphasis on the present moment. In our fast-paced and often chaotic lives, it is easy to become preoccupied with thoughts about the past or worries about the future. This constant mental chatter can lead to feelings of anxiety, stress, and overwhelm. Mindfulness encourages us to bring our attention back to the present, allowing us to fully experience and engage with whatever is happening right now. By focusing on the here and now, we can reduce the impact of negative thoughts and emotions that are tied to past regrets or future anxieties. This shift in focus can create a sense of calm and clarity, helping us to respond to life's challenges with greater equanimity.

The practice of mindfulness involves several key components, including awareness, acceptance, and non-judgment. Awareness is the act of paying attention to our thoughts, emotions, sensations, and surroundings. This heightened state of awareness allows us to observe our inner and outer experiences without becoming entangled in them. Acceptance involves acknowledging our thoughts and feelings as they are, without trying to change or suppress them. This does not mean that we condone or approve of all our thoughts and emotions, but rather that we recognize their presence without resistance. Non-judgment refers to the practice of observing our experiences without labeling them as good or bad, right or wrong. By suspending judgment, we can create a more compassionate and understanding relationship with ourselves and others.

Mindfulness can be practiced in various ways, ranging from formal meditation to informal daily activities. One of the most common forms of mindfulness practice is mindfulness meditation. This involves setting aside time to sit quietly and focus on the breath, bodily sensations, or other points of focus. The goal is not to achieve a state of complete stillness or to eliminate all thoughts, but rather to observe the flow of thoughts and sensations with a sense of openness and curiosity. When the mind inevitably wanders, the practice involves gently bringing the attention back to the chosen point of focus, without self-criticism or frustration. Over time, this practice can strengthen our ability to maintain present-moment awareness and cultivate a more balanced and centered state of mind.

In addition to formal meditation, mindfulness can be integrated into everyday activities such as eating, walking, and even washing dishes. These informal practices involve bringing mindful awareness to the task at hand, fully engaging with the sensory experiences and movements involved. For example, mindful eating involves savoring each bite of food, paying attention to the flavors, textures, and sensations in the mouth. By slowing down and focusing on the present moment, we can enhance our enjoyment of everyday activities and reduce the tendency to rush through life on autopilot.

One of the most significant benefits of mindfulness is its ability to reduce stress. Research has shown that mindfulness practices can lower levels of cortisol, the body's primary stress hormone, and decrease symptoms of anxiety and depression. By bringing our attention to the present moment, we can break the cycle of rumination and worry that often exacerbates stress. Mindfulness also helps to activate the body's relaxation response, promoting a state of calm and relaxation. This can be particularly beneficial in today's high-stress world, where many people struggle with chronic stress and its associated health problems.

Mindfulness can also enhance our emotional regulation and resilience. By observing our thoughts and emotions without judgment, we can create a space between stimulus and response. This space allows us to respond to difficult situations with greater clarity and wisdom, rather than reacting impulsively out of habit or emotion. Mindfulness helps us to recognize and understand our emotional patterns, giving us the tools to manage our emotions more effectively. This can lead to greater emotional stability and a reduced likelihood of being overwhelmed by intense feelings.

The practice of mindfulness also fosters greater self-awareness and self-acceptance. By paying attention to our inner experiences, we can gain deeper insights into our thoughts, beliefs, and behaviors. This self-awareness can help us to identify and challenge unhelpful patterns and to cultivate a more positive and compassionate relationship with ourselves. Self-acceptance involves recognizing and embracing our imperfections and vulnerabilities, allowing us to let go of self-criticism and judgment. This can lead to greater self-confidence and a sense of inner peace.

Mindfulness can have a positive impact on our relationships as well. By cultivating present-moment awareness and non-judgment, we can become more attuned to the needs and emotions of others. This can enhance our ability to listen deeply and respond with empathy and compassion. Mindfulness helps us to be fully present with our loved ones, fostering deeper connections and more meaningful interactions. It can also reduce reactivity and defensiveness, helping us to navigate conflicts and challenges with greater skill and understanding.

In addition to its psychological benefits, mindfulness can also improve physical health. Research has shown that mindfulness practices can lower blood pressure, improve sleep quality, and boost immune function. By reducing stress and promoting relaxation, mindfulness can support the body's natural healing processes and enhance overall well-being. Mindfulness can also encourage healthier lifestyle choices, such as mindful eating and regular physical activity, which can contribute to long-term health and vitality.

Mindfulness can be particularly beneficial for individuals dealing with chronic pain or illness. By bringing attention to the present moment, mindfulness can help individuals to manage their symptoms and reduce the impact of pain on their daily lives. Mindfulness encourages a non-judgmental awareness of physical sensations, which can help to reduce the emotional distress associated with pain. It can also promote a greater sense of acceptance and resilience, helping individuals to navigate the challenges of living with a chronic condition.

The practice of mindfulness is not limited to individuals; it can also be applied in various settings, such as schools, workplaces, and healthcare environments. In schools, mindfulness programs have been shown to improve students' focus, emotional regulation, and overall well-being. By teaching mindfulness skills to children and adolescents, we can help them to develop healthy coping mechanisms and build a foundation for lifelong resilience. In the workplace, mindfulness can enhance employee well-being, reduce stress, and improve productivity and job satisfaction. Mindfulness training can also promote a more positive and collaborative work environment, fostering better communication and teamwork. In healthcare settings, mindfulness-based interventions can support patient care and improve health outcomes. Healthcare providers who practice mindfulness may also experience reduced burnout and increased job satisfaction, allowing them to provide more compassionate and effective care.

Despite its many benefits, mindfulness is not a quick fix or a cure-all. It requires consistent practice and a willingness to engage with the present moment, even when it is uncomfortable or challenging. Mindfulness is a skill that develops over time, and its effects can become more pronounced with regular practice. It is important to approach mindfulness with an open and non-striving attitude, allowing the practice to unfold naturally and without pressure.

For those new to mindfulness, it can be helpful to start with short and simple practices. Guided meditations, mindfulness apps, and classes can provide structured support and guidance. It can also be beneficial to find a mindfulness community or group, where individuals can share their experiences and support each other's practice. As mindfulness becomes more integrated into daily life, individuals may find that they naturally incorporate mindfulness into a broader range of activities and experiences.

Mindfulness is a deeply personal practice, and its benefits can extend beyond individual well-being to encompass broader aspects of life and society. By cultivating mindfulness, we can develop a greater sense of interconnectedness and compassion for others. This can inspire us to act with greater kindness and empathy, contributing to a more just and harmonious world. Mindfulness can also foster a sense of gratitude and appreciation for the present moment, helping us to live more fully and authentically.

In conclusion, mindfulness plays a crucial role in enhancing our overall well-being and personal growth. By cultivating present-moment awareness, acceptance, and non-judgment, mindfulness helps us to reduce stress, regulate our emotions, and improve our relationships. It fosters greater self-awareness and self-acceptance, and it can have significant benefits for our physical health. Mindfulness can be practiced in various ways, from formal meditation to informal daily activities, and its effects can become more pronounced with regular practice. While mindfulness is not a quick fix, its consistent practice can lead to profound and lasting changes in our lives. By embracing mindfulness, we can navigate the complexities of modern living with greater ease, resilience, and compassion, and create a more fulfilling and meaningful life.

"Self-compassion is the practice of treating ourselves with kindness and understanding, especially in times of difficulty. It allows us to embrace our imperfections without judgment. With self-compassion, we build a foundation of inner strength."

NINE

REWRITING YOUR STORY

Rewriting your story is a powerful and transformative process that involves changing the narrative you tell yourself about your life. Our personal narratives shape our identity, influence our behavior, and determine how we interact with the world. They are the stories we create to make sense of our experiences, and they can either empower us or limit us. Often, these narratives are shaped by past events, societal expectations, and internalized beliefs. By consciously rewriting our story, we can reclaim our power, redefine our identity, and create a more fulfilling and authentic life.

The first step in rewriting your story is to become aware of the current narrative you are living by. This involves examining the stories you tell yourself about who you are, what you are capable of, and what your life means. These stories are often rooted in past experiences, and they can be influenced by family, culture, and societal norms. Identifying these narratives requires self-reflection and honesty. It involves recognizing the patterns and themes that recur in your thoughts and understanding how they affect your emotions and behavior.

Once you have identified your current narrative, the next step is to challenge and question it. Ask yourself whether the story you are telling is true, accurate, and helpful. Often, our narratives are filled with limiting beliefs and negative self-talk that hold us back. For example, you might believe that you are not good enough, that you will never succeed, or that you are defined by past mistakes. These beliefs can become self-fulfilling prophecies, as they shape your actions and attitudes. Challenging these beliefs involves questioning their validity and considering alternative perspectives. It requires asking yourself whether these beliefs are based on facts or assumptions and whether they serve your best interests.

Rewriting your story also involves reframing your experiences. This means looking at past events from a different perspective and finding new meanings in them. Instead of viewing a failure as a reflection of your worth, you can see it as a learning opportunity that helped you grow and develop resilience. Instead of seeing a difficult experience as something that broke you, you can view it as something that shaped your strength and character. Reframing allows you to transform negative experiences into sources of wisdom and empowerment.

Another important aspect of rewriting your story is letting go of the victim mentality. This involves taking responsibility for your life and your choices, rather than blaming others or external circumstances for your situation. While it is important to acknowledge the impact of external factors, it is equally important to recognize your own agency and power. Taking responsibility means understanding that you have the ability to shape your narrative and create the life you want. It involves shifting from a mindset of helplessness to one of empowerment and possibility.

Creating a new narrative requires envisioning the life you want to live and the person you want to become. This involves setting clear and specific goals and identifying the values and principles that are important to you. Your new story should reflect your true desires, aspirations, and strengths. It should be a story that inspires and motivates you, and one that aligns with your authentic self. Envisioning your new story involves using your imagination and creativity to picture the life you want in vivid detail. It can be helpful to write down your new narrative or create a vision board that represents your goals and dreams.

As you rewrite your story, it is important to take concrete actions that support your new narrative. This involves making changes in your behavior, habits, and attitudes that align with the life you want to create. It may involve setting new routines, seeking out new opportunities, and building new skills. Taking action is essential for turning your new narrative into reality. It demonstrates your commitment to your new story and reinforces your belief in your ability to create change.

Rewriting your story also involves surrounding yourself with supportive people who believe in you and your vision. Positive relationships can provide encouragement, inspiration, and accountability as you work towards your goals. Seek out individuals who uplift and empower you, and distance yourself from those who undermine or doubt your abilities. Building a strong support network can help you stay motivated and focused on your new narrative.

Mindfulness and self-awareness are important tools for rewriting your story. By practicing mindfulness, you can become more aware of your thoughts and emotions, and how they influence your behavior. Mindfulness allows you to observe your internal dialogue without judgment and to identify any negative patterns that may be holding you back. Self-awareness helps you understand your strengths and weaknesses, and how they contribute to your narrative. By cultivating mindfulness and self-awareness, you can make more conscious and intentional choices that align with your new story.

Forgiveness is another crucial aspect of rewriting your story. This includes forgiving yourself for past mistakes and forgiving others who may have hurt you. Holding onto anger, resentment, and guilt can keep you trapped in your old narrative. Forgiveness allows you to release these negative emotions and create space for healing and growth. It involves letting go of the past and focusing on the present and future. Forgiveness is a powerful act of self-compassion and liberation that can transform your narrative and your life.

Building resilience is essential for maintaining your new narrative, especially when faced with challenges and setbacks. Resilience involves developing the ability to bounce back from adversity and to stay focused on your goals. It requires a positive mindset, effective coping strategies, and a strong support system. Building resilience involves practicing self-care, maintaining a healthy lifestyle, and seeking out opportunities for growth and learning. By cultivating resilience, you can navigate obstacles with greater ease and continue to move forward with your new narrative.

Celebrating your successes and milestones is an important part of reinforcing your new story. Acknowledging your achievements, no matter how small, can boost your confidence and motivation. Celebrations provide an opportunity to reflect on your progress and to appreciate how far you have come. They remind you that you are capable of creating positive change and that your new narrative is becoming a reality. Whether it's treating yourself to something special, sharing your accomplishments with loved ones, or simply taking a moment to savor your success, celebrating your achievements can help you stay inspired and committed to your new story.

Gratitude is a powerful practice that can enhance your new narrative. By cultivating gratitude, you can shift your focus from what is lacking or negative in your life to what is abundant and positive. Gratitude helps you appreciate the present moment and recognize the blessings and opportunities that surround you. Keeping a gratitude journal, expressing thanks to others, and savoring positive experiences are all ways to practice gratitude. By incorporating gratitude into your daily life, you can create a more positive and fulfilling narrative.

Ultimately, rewriting your story is about reclaiming your power and living authentically. It involves letting go of limiting beliefs and negative self-talk, and embracing a new narrative that reflects your true self. It requires courage, commitment, and a willingness to take risks. Rewriting your story is a continuous process of growth and self-discovery. It involves being open to change, learning from your experiences, and continually evolving your narrative to align with your goals and values.

In conclusion, rewriting your story is a transformative process that involves changing the narrative you tell yourself about your life. It requires self-reflection, challenging limiting beliefs, and reframing your experiences. It involves taking responsibility for your life, envisioning your new narrative, and taking concrete actions to support it. Surrounding yourself with supportive people, practicing mindfulness and self-awareness, and cultivating forgiveness and resilience are all important aspects of this process. Celebrating your successes and practicing gratitude can reinforce your new narrative and create a more positive and fulfilling life. Rewriting your story is about reclaiming your power, living authentically, and creating the life you truly desire. It is a journey of self-discovery and growth that can lead to profound and lasting change.

ϷϷϷ

"Gratitude shifts our focus from what we lack to what we have. It is the practice of appreciating the positive aspects of our lives. Through gratitude, we cultivate a sense of contentment and abundance."

TEN

THE IMPACT OF TRAUMA

Trauma has a profound impact on individuals, affecting their mental, emotional, and physical well-being. It can result from various distressing experiences, such as abuse, violence, accidents, natural disasters, or any event that overwhelms a person's ability to cope. The effects of trauma can be long-lasting and pervasive, influencing how individuals perceive themselves, others, and the world around them. Understanding the impact of trauma is essential for healing and recovery, as it helps individuals recognize the sources of their distress and seek appropriate support and treatment.

One of the most significant impacts of trauma is on mental health. Traumatic experiences can lead to a range of psychological conditions, including post-traumatic stress disorder (PTSD), anxiety disorders, and depression. PTSD is characterized by symptoms such as intrusive memories, flashbacks, nightmares, and severe anxiety, which can significantly impair daily functioning. Individuals with PTSD may also experience hypervigilance, an exaggerated startle response, and avoidance of reminders of the trauma. These symptoms can make it difficult to engage in normal activities and maintain relationships.

Anxiety disorders, such as generalized anxiety disorder and panic disorder, are also common among individuals who have experienced trauma. These conditions are marked by excessive worry, fear, and physical symptoms such as rapid heartbeat, sweating, and shortness of breath. Trauma can create a persistent sense of danger and threat, leading to chronic anxiety and difficulty relaxing. Depression is another common outcome of trauma, characterized by persistent sadness, hopelessness, and a lack of interest in previously enjoyed activities. Depression can also lead to physical symptoms such as fatigue, changes in appetite, and sleep disturbances.

The emotional impact of trauma is profound and multifaceted. Trauma can disrupt an individual's sense of self and emotional stability, leading to feelings of shame, guilt, and worthlessness. These emotions are often rooted in self-blame, where individuals believe they could have prevented the traumatic event or that it was somehow their fault. This internalized guilt and shame can be particularly damaging, as it undermines self-esteem and self-worth. Trauma can also create a sense of disconnection from oneself and others, leading to feelings of isolation and loneliness. Individuals may struggle to trust others and form meaningful relationships, fearing that they will be hurt or betrayed again.

Trauma can also have a significant impact on physical health. The body's response to trauma involves the activation of the stress response system, which releases hormones such as cortisol and adrenaline. While this response is adaptive in the short term, chronic activation due to unresolved trauma can lead to a range of physical health problems. These can include chronic pain, gastrointestinal issues, cardiovascular problems, and a weakened immune system. Additionally, trauma can lead to unhealthy coping mechanisms, such as substance abuse, which can further harm physical health.

Cognitive functioning can also be affected by trauma. Individuals may experience difficulties with concentration, memory, and decision-making. This cognitive impairment is often a result of the brain's response to trauma, which can alter neural pathways and affect brain regions involved in these functions. For example, the hippocampus, which is responsible for memory formation, can be negatively impacted by high levels of stress hormones. This can lead to memory problems and difficulties in learning new information. The prefrontal cortex, which is involved in decision-making and impulse control, can also be affected, leading to challenges in managing emotions and behaviors.

The impact of trauma extends to social and relational aspects of life. Traumatized individuals may withdraw from social interactions and isolate themselves from others. This isolation can be a protective mechanism to avoid triggers and potential harm, but it also prevents individuals from receiving support and building healthy relationships. Trauma can also affect how individuals relate to others, leading to difficulties in communication, trust, and intimacy. Relationships may become strained or dysfunctional, as individuals struggle to navigate their emotions and reactions. This can result in a cycle of conflict, misunderstanding, and further isolation.

Trauma can also affect an individual's sense of safety and control. The experience of trauma often involves a loss of control and a sense of helplessness. This can lead to a pervasive feeling of insecurity and a heightened need for control in other areas of life. Individuals may become overly cautious or avoidant, seeking to minimize the risk of further harm. This hypervigilance and need for control can be exhausting and limit opportunities for growth and new experiences. It can also reinforce a negative worldview, where the world is seen as inherently dangerous and unpredictable.

Healing from trauma is a complex and multifaceted process that requires time, support, and effective therapeutic interventions. One of the most important steps in healing is acknowledging and validating the trauma. This involves recognizing the impact of the traumatic experience and understanding that the resulting feelings and behaviors are normal responses to abnormal events. Validation from supportive individuals, such as friends, family, or therapists, can help individuals feel understood and less alone in their struggles.

Therapy is a crucial component of trauma recovery. Various therapeutic approaches can be effective, including cognitive-behavioral therapy (CBT), eye movement desensitization and reprocessing (EMDR), and somatic experiencing. CBT helps individuals identify and challenge negative thought patterns and beliefs related to the trauma, and develop healthier ways of thinking and coping. EMDR is a specialized therapy that uses bilateral stimulation to help individuals process and integrate traumatic memories. Somatic experiencing focuses on the body's physical response to trauma and helps individuals release stored tension and trauma-related sensations.

Mindfulness and relaxation techniques can also be beneficial in trauma recovery. Mindfulness involves paying attention to the present moment with curiosity and non-judgment. It can help individuals become more aware of their thoughts and emotions, and develop a greater sense of control over their reactions. Relaxation techniques, such as deep breathing, progressive muscle relaxation, and meditation, can help reduce the physical symptoms of stress and promote a sense of calm and relaxation.

Building a strong support network is essential for healing from trauma. Supportive relationships provide emotional validation, encouragement, and a sense of connection. Friends, family, support groups, and therapists can all play a role in offering support and understanding. It is important for individuals to communicate their needs and boundaries to their support network, as this helps others provide the appropriate level of support. Peer support groups, where individuals with similar experiences can share and support each other, can be particularly helpful in reducing feelings of isolation and fostering a sense of community.

Self-care is another important aspect of trauma recovery. This involves taking steps to nurture and care for oneself physically, emotionally, and mentally. Self-care can include activities such as exercise, healthy eating, adequate sleep, and engaging in hobbies and activities that bring joy and relaxation. It also involves setting boundaries and prioritizing one's own needs, which can help prevent burnout and promote resilience.

Resilience is the ability to bounce back from adversity and maintain a sense of well-being despite challenges. Building resilience involves developing effective coping strategies, fostering positive relationships, and maintaining a hopeful and optimistic outlook. Resilience can be cultivated through practices such as gratitude, positive self-talk, and seeking out opportunities for growth and learning. By building resilience, individuals can better navigate the ups and downs of the healing process and continue to move forward.

Forgiveness is another important component of trauma recovery. This includes both forgiving oneself for any perceived shortcomings or mistakes, and forgiving others who may have caused harm. Forgiveness is not about condoning or excusing harmful behavior, but about releasing the hold that anger and resentment have on one's life. It is a process of letting go that allows individuals to move forward with a lighter heart and a greater sense of peace. Self-forgiveness involves recognizing one's own humanity and imperfections, and offering oneself the same compassion and understanding that one would offer to a friend.

Creative expression can also be a powerful tool for healing from trauma. Art, music, writing, and other forms of creative expression allow individuals to process and release their emotions in a non-verbal and intuitive way. These activities can provide a sense of accomplishment and joy, helping to shift focus from pain to creativity and self-expression. Creative expression can also help individuals explore and make sense of their experiences, and find new ways to communicate their feelings and stories.

It is important to recognize that healing from trauma is a gradual and ongoing process. There may be times when progress feels slow or setbacks occur, and it is important to approach these moments with patience and self-compassion. Healing is not a linear journey, and each person's path to recovery is unique. By consistently practicing the strategies outlined above, individuals can gradually release the hold of trauma and create a more positive and empowering relationship with themselves and the world.

In conclusion, the impact of trauma is profound and far-reaching, affecting mental, emotional, and physical well-being. Trauma can lead to conditions such as PTSD, anxiety, and depression, and can disrupt cognitive functioning, relationships, and one's sense of safety and control. Healing from trauma requires acknowledging and validating the trauma, seeking therapeutic support, and building a strong support network. Practices such as mindfulness, self-care, and creative expression can also support the healing process. By cultivating resilience, practicing forgiveness, and approaching the journey with patience and self-compassion, individuals can heal from trauma and create a more fulfilling and empowered life. Understanding the impact of trauma and taking proactive steps towards recovery is essential for achieving long-term well-being and personal growth.

ݒݒݒ

"Setting healthy boundaries protects our well-being and ensures our needs are respected. It is an act of self-respect and self-care. With boundaries, we create space for personal growth and fulfillment."

ELEVEN

BUILDING RESILIENCE

Building resilience is a crucial aspect of personal development that allows individuals to navigate life's challenges with greater ease and strength. Resilience is the ability to bounce back from adversity, adapt to change, and continue moving forward in the face of difficulties. It is not an innate trait but a skill that can be developed and strengthened over time through conscious effort and practice. Understanding how to build resilience can empower individuals to handle stress, overcome obstacles, and thrive in both personal and professional life.

Resilience begins with self-awareness, which involves understanding one's own thoughts, emotions, and behaviors. Self-awareness helps individuals recognize how they respond to stress and adversity, allowing them to identify patterns that may be counterproductive. By becoming more aware of their emotional triggers and responses, individuals can develop strategies to manage their reactions more effectively. This awareness can also help them identify their strengths and areas for growth, providing a foundation for building resilience.

Another fundamental aspect of resilience is a positive mindset. A positive mindset involves viewing challenges as opportunities for growth rather than insurmountable obstacles. It requires shifting from a fixed mindset, which sees abilities as static and unchangeable, to a growth mindset, which believes that abilities can be developed through effort and learning. This shift in perspective can transform how individuals approach difficulties, encouraging them to persevere and find solutions rather than giving up in the face of setbacks.

Developing strong problem-solving skills is essential for resilience. Problem-solving involves identifying the root cause of a problem, generating possible solutions, and implementing the most effective one. This process requires critical thinking, creativity, and flexibility. By honing these skills, individuals can tackle challenges more effectively and feel more confident in their ability to handle future difficulties. Practicing problem-solving in everyday situations can strengthen these skills and make them more accessible during times of crisis.

Building and maintaining a strong support network is another key component of resilience. Supportive relationships provide emotional validation, encouragement, and practical assistance during difficult times. Friends, family, colleagues, and mentors can offer different perspectives and advice, helping individuals navigate challenges more effectively. Being part of a supportive community also fosters a sense of belonging and connection, which can be a powerful buffer against stress and adversity. It is important for individuals to nurture these relationships and to seek support when needed, rather than trying to handle everything on their own.

Resilience also involves effective stress management. Chronic stress can deplete physical and emotional resources, making it harder to cope with adversity. Developing healthy coping mechanisms for managing stress is crucial for building resilience. These mechanisms can include regular physical activity, relaxation techniques, and hobbies that bring joy and relaxation. Physical activity, such as walking, running, or yoga, can reduce stress hormones and improve mood. Relaxation techniques, such as deep breathing, meditation, and progressive muscle relaxation, can help calm the mind and body. Engaging in hobbies and activities that bring pleasure can provide a mental break from stress and foster a sense of well-being.

Mindfulness is a powerful tool for building resilience. Mindfulness involves paying attention to the present moment with curiosity and non-judgment. It helps individuals become more aware of their thoughts, emotions, and physical sensations, allowing them to respond to stress with greater clarity and calm. Mindfulness practices, such as meditation, mindful breathing, and mindful movement, can reduce stress, enhance emotional regulation, and increase overall resilience. By cultivating mindfulness, individuals can develop a greater sense of control over their reactions and a more balanced perspective on challenges.

Cultivating emotional regulation is essential for resilience. Emotional regulation involves managing and responding to emotions in healthy ways. It requires recognizing and understanding one's emotions, expressing them appropriately, and using strategies to modulate their intensity. Techniques such as cognitive reappraisal, which involves reframing negative thoughts to reduce their emotional impact, and emotion-focused coping, which involves addressing the emotional response to a stressor, can enhance emotional regulation. By developing these skills, individuals can navigate emotional challenges more effectively and maintain their well-being during difficult times.

Setting realistic and achievable goals is another important aspect of building resilience. Goals provide direction and purpose, helping individuals stay focused and motivated. Breaking down larger goals into smaller, manageable steps can make them more attainable and reduce feelings of overwhelm. It is also important to set goals that are aligned with one's values and priorities, as this can enhance motivation and commitment. By setting and working towards meaningful goals, individuals can build a sense of accomplishment and resilience.

Developing a sense of purpose and meaning is crucial for resilience. A sense of purpose provides motivation and direction, helping individuals persevere through challenges. It involves understanding one's values, passions, and long-term aspirations, and aligning actions with these guiding principles. Engaging in activities that are meaningful and fulfilling, such as volunteering, pursuing hobbies, or contributing to a cause, can enhance a sense of purpose. By cultivating a sense of purpose, individuals can maintain a positive outlook and resilience in the face of adversity.

Practicing gratitude is a powerful way to build resilience. Gratitude involves recognizing and appreciating the positive aspects of life, even in the midst of challenges. Keeping a gratitude journal, where one regularly writes down things they are thankful for, can enhance this practice. Expressing gratitude to others, whether through words or actions, can also strengthen relationships and foster a positive mindset. By focusing on the positive, individuals can shift their perspective and build a more resilient outlook on life.

Learning from past experiences is essential for building resilience. Reflecting on previous challenges and identifying what strategies were effective can provide valuable insights for future situations. It involves recognizing the lessons learned from adversity and applying them to new challenges. This reflection can also help individuals build confidence in their ability to overcome difficulties. By viewing past experiences as opportunities for growth, individuals can develop a more resilient mindset.

Resilience also involves being adaptable and flexible. Life is unpredictable, and the ability to adapt to changing circumstances is crucial for navigating challenges. Flexibility involves being open to new ideas, approaches, and solutions, and adjusting plans as needed. It requires letting go of rigid expectations and embracing uncertainty. By cultivating adaptability, individuals can respond to change with greater ease and resilience.

Self-compassion is another important aspect of resilience. Self-compassion involves treating oneself with kindness and understanding during times of difficulty. It means recognizing that everyone experiences setbacks and challenges, and offering oneself the same compassion and support that one would offer to a friend. Self-compassion can reduce self-criticism and enhance emotional well-being. By practicing self-compassion, individuals can build resilience and maintain a positive self-image during tough times.

Resilience also involves maintaining a healthy lifestyle. Physical health and well-being are closely connected to emotional resilience. Regular exercise, a balanced diet, adequate sleep, and avoiding harmful substances are all important for maintaining physical health. Taking care of one's body can enhance energy levels, improve mood, and increase the ability to cope with stress. By prioritizing physical health, individuals can build a strong foundation for resilience.

Finally, resilience involves a commitment to continuous learning and growth. Embracing a mindset of lifelong learning can enhance adaptability and problem-solving skills. It involves seeking out new experiences, acquiring new knowledge and skills, and being open to feedback and self-improvement. This commitment to growth can enhance confidence and resilience, as individuals develop a broader range of tools and strategies for navigating challenges. By continuously learning and growing, individuals can build a more resilient and fulfilling life.

In conclusion, building resilience is a multifaceted process that involves developing self-awareness, cultivating a positive mindset, and honing problem-solving skills. It requires building and maintaining a strong support network, managing stress effectively, and practicing mindfulness and emotional regulation. Setting realistic goals, developing a sense of purpose, practicing gratitude, and learning from past experiences are also crucial components of resilience. Adaptability, self-compassion, a healthy lifestyle, and a commitment to continuous learning further enhance resilience. By integrating these strategies into daily life, individuals can build the strength and resilience needed to navigate life's challenges and thrive in both personal and professional domains. Resilience is not a fixed trait but a dynamic skill that can be developed and strengthened over time, empowering individuals to face adversity with greater ease and confidence.

"Rewriting our story means transforming the narrative we tell ourselves about our lives. It is the power to change limiting beliefs into empowering ones. Through this process, we create a life that reflects our true potential."

TWELVE
SEEKING CLOSURE

Seeking closure is an essential process in dealing with unresolved issues and moving forward in life. Closure refers to the resolution of emotional or psychological pain from past events, relationships, or experiences that continue to affect us. It involves understanding, accepting, and integrating these experiences into our lives in a way that allows us to let go of the pain and find peace. The journey to closure can be complex and deeply personal, but it is crucial for emotional well-being and personal growth.

One of the first steps in seeking closure is acknowledging the unresolved issue and recognizing its impact on your life. This requires honesty and self-reflection. Unresolved issues often manifest as recurring thoughts, persistent feelings of sadness or anger, or an inability to move forward in certain areas of life. Identifying these patterns is the first step toward addressing them. It involves admitting that something from the past is still affecting you and that it needs attention.

Once you have acknowledged the unresolved issue, the next step is to understand it. This involves exploring the circumstances and emotions surrounding the event or relationship. Understanding why something happened, how it affected you, and what you can learn from it is crucial. This process often involves revisiting painful memories and emotions, which can be challenging but necessary for healing. It may be helpful to write about your experiences in a journal, talk with a trusted friend or therapist, or engage in other reflective practices that allow you to process your thoughts and feelings.

Acceptance is a key component of seeking closure. Acceptance does not mean condoning or approving of what happened, but rather acknowledging the reality of the situation and your feelings about it. It involves letting go of any desire to change the past and recognizing that you cannot control what has already happened. Acceptance allows you to release the grip of the past on your present and future. It is about coming to terms with the fact that some questions may never be answered and some aspects of the situation may never be fully understood.

Forgiveness often plays a significant role in seeking closure. This includes forgiving others who may have hurt you and forgiving yourself for any perceived mistakes or shortcomings. Forgiveness is not about excusing or forgetting the wrongdoing, but about freeing yourself from the burden of anger, resentment, and blame. It is a process of letting go that allows you to move forward with a lighter heart. Self-forgiveness involves recognizing your humanity and imperfections and offering yourself the same compassion and understanding you would offer to a friend. It is about acknowledging that you did the best you could with the knowledge and resources you had at the time.

Another important aspect of seeking closure is finding meaning in the experience. This involves reflecting on what you have learned and how you have grown as a result of the situation. Every experience, no matter how painful, can offer valuable lessons and insights. By finding meaning in the experience, you can transform it from a source of pain into a source of wisdom and strength. This perspective can help you integrate the experience into your life in a positive way and move forward with a greater sense of purpose and resilience.

Rituals and symbolic acts can also be helpful in seeking closure. These rituals can provide a sense of finality and allow you to formally acknowledge the end of a chapter in your life. They can be simple or elaborate, personal or communal, depending on what feels right for you. Examples of closure rituals include writing a letter to the person involved (whether or not you send it), creating a piece of art that represents your feelings, or holding a small ceremony to say goodbye to the past. These acts can help you process your emotions and create a tangible way to mark the transition.

Seeking closure often involves setting boundaries. This can mean establishing physical, emotional, or mental boundaries to protect yourself from further harm or to create the space you need to heal. It may involve limiting or cutting off contact with people who are toxic or remind you of the painful event. Setting boundaries can also mean giving yourself permission to take a break from thinking about the issue and focusing on other aspects of your life. Boundaries help create a safe environment for healing and allow you to regain control over your life.

Support from others is invaluable in the process of seeking closure. Friends, family, therapists, and support groups can provide empathy, understanding, and encouragement. Talking about your experiences and feelings with trusted individuals can help you feel less alone and more validated. They can offer different perspectives and insights that you may not have considered and can provide practical advice and support. It is important to communicate your needs and boundaries to your support network, as they may not always know how to help unless you express yourself clearly.

Self-care is another crucial aspect of seeking closure. Taking care of your physical, emotional, and mental well-being is essential for healing. This includes activities such as exercise, healthy eating, adequate sleep, and engaging in hobbies and activities that bring you joy and relaxation. Self-care also involves being gentle with yourself and allowing yourself to feel your emotions without judgment. It means recognizing that healing is a process and that it is okay to take time for yourself and prioritize your needs.

Mindfulness can be a powerful tool in the journey to closure. Mindfulness involves paying attention to the present moment with curiosity and non-judgment. It helps you become more aware of your thoughts and emotions, allowing you to observe them without becoming overwhelmed. Mindfulness practices, such as meditation, deep breathing, and mindful movement, can reduce stress and increase emotional regulation. By cultivating mindfulness, you can create a sense of calm and clarity that supports the process of seeking closure.

Another important aspect of seeking closure is focusing on the future. While it is important to understand and accept the past, it is equally important to envision and work towards a positive future. Setting goals and creating a vision for your life can help you move forward with purpose and direction. This involves identifying what you want to achieve, what brings you joy, and what steps you need to take to create the life you desire. By focusing on the future, you can shift your energy from dwelling on the past to building a fulfilling and meaningful life.

Resilience is a key factor in seeking closure. Resilience is the ability to bounce back from adversity and continue moving forward despite challenges. It involves developing effective coping strategies, fostering positive relationships, and maintaining a hopeful and optimistic outlook. Resilience can be built through practices such as gratitude, positive self-talk, and seeking out opportunities for growth and learning. By building resilience, you can navigate the ups and downs of the closure process and continue to move forward with strength and determination.

Seeking closure is not a one-time event but an ongoing process. There may be times when feelings of pain or sadness resurface, and it is important to approach these moments with patience and self-compassion. Healing is not a linear journey, and setbacks are a natural part of the process. By consistently practicing the strategies outlined above, you can gradually release the hold of the past and create a more positive and empowering relationship with yourself.

In conclusion, seeking closure is a deeply personal and transformative process that involves understanding, accepting, and integrating past experiences into your life in a way that allows you to move forward with peace and resilience. It requires acknowledging the unresolved issue, exploring its impact, and finding meaning in the experience. Acceptance, forgiveness, rituals, and setting boundaries are all important components of seeking closure. Support from others, self-care, mindfulness, and focusing on the future can further support the process. Building resilience and approaching the journey with patience and self-compassion are crucial for achieving long-term well-being and personal growth. By seeking closure, you can free yourself from the pain of the past and create a more fulfilling and empowered life.

ppp

"Letting go of guilt involves releasing the burdens of past mistakes. It is about understanding that we did our best with the knowledge we had. By letting go, we open ourselves to growth and new possibilities."

THIRTEEN

CREATING HEALTHY BOUNDARIES

Creating healthy boundaries is a fundamental aspect of maintaining emotional well-being and healthy relationships. Boundaries define our personal limits and communicate what we find acceptable and unacceptable in our interactions with others. They protect our physical, emotional, and mental health by ensuring that our needs and values are respected. Setting and maintaining healthy boundaries can be challenging, especially for those who are used to prioritizing others' needs over their own. However, learning to establish and uphold these boundaries is crucial for fostering self-respect, reducing stress, and creating more balanced and fulfilling relationships.

The first step in creating healthy boundaries is self-awareness. This involves understanding your own needs, values, and limits. Reflecting on past experiences can help you identify situations where you felt uncomfortable, disrespected, or overwhelmed. These instances can provide insight into the boundaries that need to be set. It is important to recognize that boundaries are personal and unique to each individual. What feels acceptable to one person may not feel the same to another. Understanding your own preferences and limits is key to establishing boundaries that are right for you.

Once you have identified your boundaries, the next step is to communicate them clearly and assertively. Effective communication is essential for setting boundaries, as it ensures that others understand your needs and expectations. This involves expressing your boundaries in a calm and respectful manner, without apology or justification. For example, if you need time alone to recharge, you might say, "I need some quiet time for myself this evening. Let's catch up tomorrow." It is important to be specific and direct, as vague or ambiguous statements can lead to misunderstandings.

Asserting boundaries can be challenging, especially if you are not used to doing so. It may feel uncomfortable or even confrontational at first. However, it is important to remember that setting boundaries is a form of self-care and self-respect. It is not about rejecting or punishing others, but about protecting your own well-being. Practicing assertiveness can help you develop the confidence to uphold your boundaries. This involves standing firm in your decisions, even if others do not agree or understand. It is important to remain calm and composed, and to avoid becoming defensive or aggressive.

In addition to verbal communication, non-verbal cues can also play a role in setting boundaries. Body language, tone of voice, and facial expressions can all convey your feelings and intentions. For example, maintaining eye contact and using a steady tone of voice can reinforce your message and show that you are serious about your boundaries. Non-verbal cues can also help you assert your boundaries in situations where verbal communication may not be possible or appropriate.

Another important aspect of creating healthy boundaries is consistency. This involves consistently enforcing your boundaries and not allowing exceptions or compromises that undermine them.

Inconsistent boundaries can lead to confusion and may encourage others to disregard your limits. It is important to stay committed to your boundaries, even if it feels difficult or inconvenient. Consistency reinforces your boundaries and helps others understand that they are non-negotiable.

Setting boundaries also involves being prepared for resistance or pushback from others. Some people may not respond positively to your boundaries, especially if they are used to you accommodating their needs. They may try to test or challenge your limits, or they may express frustration or disappointment. It is important to remain firm and to reiterate your boundaries as needed. You can acknowledge their feelings while still standing by your decisions. For example, you might say, "I understand that you are upset, but I need to prioritize my own well-being right now."

Boundaries are not only about saying no to others, but also about saying yes to yourself. This involves prioritizing your own needs and self-care. It means giving yourself permission to rest, to take breaks, and to engage in activities that bring you joy and fulfillment. Self-care is an essential component of maintaining healthy boundaries, as it helps you recharge and build resilience. By taking care of yourself, you are better equipped to handle stress and to maintain your boundaries in the face of challenges.

It is also important to recognize that boundaries can change over time. As you grow and evolve, your needs and limits may shift. It is important to regularly reassess your boundaries and to adjust them as needed. This involves staying attuned to your own feelings and responses, and being willing to make changes when necessary. Flexibility is key to maintaining healthy boundaries, as it allows you to adapt to new situations and to continue prioritizing your well-being.

Boundaries are not only relevant in personal relationships but also in professional settings. In the workplace, setting boundaries can help you manage your workload, reduce stress, and prevent burnout. This may involve setting limits on your availability, such as not answering work emails outside of office hours, or delegating tasks to ensure a manageable workload. It may also involve setting boundaries with colleagues, such as not engaging in office gossip or refusing to take on additional responsibilities that are beyond your capacity. Professional boundaries help create a healthy work environment and promote work-life balance.

In family relationships, boundaries can be particularly challenging to set and maintain. Family dynamics are often complex, and there may be longstanding patterns of behavior that are difficult to change. However, setting boundaries with family members is crucial for maintaining healthy relationships and protecting your emotional well-being. This may involve setting limits on contact, such as not answering phone calls during certain times, or establishing rules for interactions, such as not discussing certain topics. It is important to communicate your boundaries clearly and to reinforce them consistently, even if it causes temporary discomfort or conflict.

In romantic relationships, boundaries are essential for maintaining mutual respect and understanding. This involves setting limits on behaviors that you find unacceptable, such as disrespectful language or invasion of privacy. It also involves establishing expectations for the relationship, such as how much time you spend together and how you handle conflicts. Healthy boundaries in romantic relationships promote trust, intimacy, and mutual support. They allow both partners to feel secure and valued, and they help prevent codependency and resentment.

Creating healthy boundaries also involves respecting the boundaries of others. Just as you have the right to set and enforce your own boundaries, so do others. This means listening to and honoring their limits, even if they differ from your own. Respecting others' boundaries fosters mutual respect and strengthens relationships. It also sets a positive example and encourages others to respect your boundaries in return.

Boundaries are an essential aspect of emotional intelligence. Emotional intelligence involves understanding and managing your own emotions, as well as recognizing and responding to the emotions of others. Setting boundaries requires a high degree of self-awareness and emotional regulation. It also involves empathy and respect for others' feelings and needs. By developing emotional intelligence, you can improve your ability to set and maintain healthy boundaries and to navigate relationships more effectively.

The process of creating healthy boundaries can be transformative. It can lead to greater self-respect, improved relationships, and a stronger sense of control over your life. It can also reduce stress and anxiety, as you learn to prioritize your well-being and to protect yourself from harmful or draining interactions. The journey to creating healthy boundaries may be challenging, but it is ultimately empowering. It allows you to take charge of your life and to create a space where you can thrive and grow.

In conclusion, creating healthy boundaries is a fundamental aspect of maintaining emotional well-being and healthy relationships. It involves understanding your own needs and limits, communicating them clearly and assertively, and consistently enforcing them. It requires self-awareness, assertiveness, and emotional regulation. Setting boundaries can be challenging, especially if you are not used to prioritizing your own needs. However, it is essential for fostering self-respect, reducing stress, and creating balanced and fulfilling relationships. By learning to set and maintain healthy boundaries, you can protect your well-being, improve your relationships, and create a more empowered and fulfilling life.

ᠵᠵᠵ

"Overcoming regret requires us to learn from our past without being defined by it. It is the courage to see each experience as a lesson. In this perspective, we find the freedom to move forward."

FOURTEEN

EMBRACING SELF-COMPASSION

Embracing self-compassion is a transformative practice that allows individuals to foster a kinder and more understanding relationship with themselves. At its core, self-compassion involves treating oneself with the same care, concern, and kindness that one would offer to a good friend. This practice is rooted in the understanding that all human beings are imperfect, that everyone makes mistakes, and that everyone experiences difficulties. Embracing self-compassion is essential for emotional well-being, personal growth, and resilience, as it helps to counteract self-criticism, reduce stress, and cultivate a sense of inner peace and acceptance.

Self-compassion consists of three main components: self-kindness, common humanity, and mindfulness. Self-kindness refers to being warm and understanding toward ourselves when we suffer, fail, or feel inadequate, rather than ignoring our pain or engaging in self-criticism. Instead of berating ourselves for our shortcomings, we offer ourselves soothing and comforting words. This aspect of self-compassion is about treating ourselves with the same care and concern that we would extend to a loved one in a similar situation.

Common humanity involves recognizing that suffering and

personal inadequacy are part of the shared human experience. Rather than feeling isolated by our failures or difficulties, we understand that everyone goes through similar challenges. This perspective helps to normalize our experiences and reduces feelings of isolation and shame. By acknowledging our common humanity, we can connect more deeply with others and feel less alone in our struggles.

Mindfulness, the third component of self-compassion, involves being present with our painful thoughts and feelings without becoming overwhelmed by them or suppressing them. It means observing our thoughts and emotions with openness and curiosity, without judgment. Mindfulness allows us to hold our experiences in a balanced awareness, giving us the space to respond to them with compassion rather than reactivity. By practicing mindfulness, we can become more aware of our inner dialogue and recognize when we are being self-critical.

One of the main barriers to self-compassion is the pervasive tendency toward self-criticism. Many people believe that self-criticism is necessary for motivation and self-improvement. They fear that if they are too kind to themselves, they will become complacent or lazy. However, research has shown that self-criticism can actually be counterproductive.

It can lead to feelings of worthlessness, anxiety, and depression, and can undermine our motivation and resilience. In contrast, self-compassion provides a supportive and encouraging environment for growth and change. When we are kind to ourselves, we are more likely to take risks, learn from our mistakes, and persist in the face of challenges.

To cultivate self-compassion, it is helpful to start by recognizing and challenging our self-critical thoughts. This involves paying attention to our inner dialogue and noticing when we are being harsh or judgmental toward ourselves. Once we become aware of these thoughts, we can question their validity and consider more compassionate alternatives.

For example, instead of thinking, "I'm such a failure," we might remind ourselves, "I did my best, and it's okay to make mistakes. I can learn from this experience." By reframing our self-critical thoughts in a more compassionate way, we can begin to change the tone of our inner dialogue and create a more supportive mindset.

Another effective practice for cultivating self-compassion is the self-compassion break. This involves taking a moment to acknowledge and respond to our suffering with kindness and understanding. The self-compassion break consists of three steps: first, we acknowledge our pain by saying something like, "This is a moment of suffering." Next, we remind ourselves of our common humanity by saying, "Suffering is a part of life. Everyone goes through difficult times."

Finally, we offer ourselves words of kindness and comfort, such as, "May I be kind to myself in this moment. May I give myself the compassion I need." This practice can be done anytime we are experiencing distress and can help to create a sense of calm and self-compassion.

Self-compassion can also be cultivated through guided meditations and mindfulness exercises. These practices help to develop awareness and kindness toward ourselves. For example, loving-kindness meditation involves directing feelings of love and compassion toward ourselves and others.

We might silently repeat phrases such as, "May I be happy. May I be healthy. May I be safe. May I live with ease." By regularly practicing loving-kindness meditation, we can strengthen our ability to offer compassion to ourselves and others.

Engaging in self-care is another important aspect of embracing self-compassion. Self-care involves taking deliberate actions to nurture and care for ourselves physically, emotionally, and mentally. This can include activities such as getting enough sleep, eating nutritious foods, exercising regularly, and engaging in hobbies and activities that bring us joy and relaxation. Self-care is not a luxury but a necessity for our well-being. By prioritizing self-care, we demonstrate to ourselves that we are worthy of care and attention.

Setting healthy boundaries is also a key component of self-compassion. Boundaries protect our well-being by ensuring that our needs and values are respected. This involves saying no to requests or demands that are unreasonable or that compromise our well-being. It also means creating space for ourselves to rest and recharge.

Setting boundaries can be challenging, especially if we are used to prioritizing others' needs over our own. However, it is essential for maintaining our emotional and physical health. By setting and maintaining healthy boundaries, we honor our own needs and create a balanced and fulfilling life.

It is important to remember that self-compassion is not about being self-indulgent or selfish. It is about recognizing our own worth and treating ourselves with the same kindness and respect that we would offer to others. Self-compassion involves balancing our own needs with the needs of others and recognizing that taking care of ourselves enables us to better care for others. It is about creating a supportive and nurturing environment within ourselves that allows us to thrive and grow.

One of the profound benefits of self-compassion is its ability to enhance our relationships with others. When we are kind and understanding toward ourselves, we are more likely to extend that same kindness and understanding to others. Self-compassion helps to reduce feelings of judgment and criticism, fostering a sense of empathy and connection.

It allows us to be more present and attentive in our interactions and to respond to others with greater compassion and support. By embracing self-compassion, we can create more harmonious and fulfilling relationships.

Self-compassion also plays a crucial role in building resilience. Life is filled with challenges and setbacks, and how we respond to these difficulties can significantly impact our well-being. Self-compassion provides a stable foundation of support and encouragement that helps us navigate adversity with greater ease.

When we treat ourselves with kindness and understanding during difficult times, we are better able to cope with stress and recover from setbacks. Self-compassion allows us to acknowledge our pain without becoming overwhelmed by it and to find the strength to move forward.

Another important aspect of self-compassion is forgiveness, both toward ourselves and others. Forgiveness involves letting go of anger, resentment, and blame and recognizing that we are all imperfect human beings. Self-forgiveness means acknowledging our mistakes and shortcomings and offering ourselves the same compassion and understanding that we would offer to a friend. It is about releasing the burden of guilt and shame and allowing ourselves to move forward with a sense of peace and acceptance.

Forgiveness of others involves recognizing that holding onto anger and resentment only perpetuates our own suffering. By offering forgiveness, we free ourselves from the negative emotions that keep us stuck in the past.

Practicing gratitude is another powerful way to embrace self-compassion. Gratitude involves recognizing and appreciating the positive aspects of our lives, even in the midst of difficulties. Keeping a gratitude journal, where we regularly write down things we are thankful for, can help to cultivate a positive and compassionate mindset.

Expressing gratitude to others, whether through words or actions, can also strengthen our relationships and enhance our sense of connection and well-being. By focusing on the positive, we can shift our perspective and create a more compassionate and fulfilling life.

In conclusion, embracing self-compassion is a transformative practice that involves treating ourselves with kindness, understanding, and respect. It requires recognizing our own worth and offering ourselves the same care and concern that we would extend to a good friend. Self-compassion is essential for emotional well-being, personal growth, and resilience. By cultivating self-compassion through practices such as mindfulness, self-care, setting boundaries, and practicing gratitude, we can create a supportive and nurturing environment within ourselves.

This, in turn, allows us to navigate life's challenges with greater ease and strength, and to build more harmonious and fulfilling relationships with others. Embracing self-compassion is a journey of self-discovery and growth that leads to a more balanced, peaceful, and empowered life.

ᗞᗞᗞ

"Healing emotional wounds is a journey of self-discovery and acceptance. It involves understanding the origins of our pain and finding ways to transform it. Through healing, we reclaim our wholeness."

FIFTEEN

THE IMPORTANCE OF SUPPORT

The importance of support in our lives cannot be overstated. Support, whether from family, friends, colleagues, or professionals, plays a critical role in our mental, emotional, and even physical well-being. It provides us with the resources, encouragement, and understanding we need to navigate life's challenges, achieve our goals, and maintain our overall health. The presence of a supportive network can make a significant difference in how we handle stress, recover from setbacks, and pursue personal and professional growth.

Human beings are inherently social creatures, and our need for connection and support is deeply ingrained. From birth, we rely on caregivers for survival and emotional security. This need for connection continues throughout our lives, shaping our relationships and interactions with others. Supportive relationships provide us with a sense of belonging and validation, helping us feel understood and valued. These connections can buffer us against the negative effects of stress and adversity, promoting resilience and well-being.

One of the primary benefits of support is the emotional validation it offers. When we share our experiences and feelings with others, we often seek empathy and understanding. Having someone listen to us, acknowledge our emotions, and offer comfort can be incredibly healing. It helps us feel less alone in our struggles and reassures us that our feelings are normal and acceptable. Emotional validation can reduce feelings of isolation and shame, fostering a sense of connection and acceptance.

Support also provides us with practical assistance and resources. In times of need, supportive individuals can offer help in various forms, such as providing advice, lending a hand with tasks, or offering financial assistance. This practical support can alleviate some of the burdens we face and make challenging situations more manageable. Knowing that we have people we can rely on for help can reduce anxiety and increase our confidence in handling difficulties.

Another crucial aspect of support is the encouragement and motivation it provides. Supportive individuals believe in our abilities and potential, often seeing strengths and possibilities that we may overlook. Their encouragement can inspire us to pursue our goals, take risks, and persist in the face of obstacles. Positive reinforcement from others can boost our self-esteem and motivation, helping us stay focused and determined. This support is particularly important during times of self-doubt or when we are facing significant challenges.

Supportive relationships also play a vital role in our physical health. Research has shown that strong social connections are associated with numerous health benefits, including lower rates of chronic illness, reduced stress levels, and improved immune function. Social support can encourage healthy behaviors, such as regular exercise, balanced nutrition, and adherence to medical advice. Additionally, the emotional benefits of support, such as reduced stress and increased feelings of well-being, can have positive effects on physical health. People with strong support networks are more likely to recover quickly from illness or injury and to maintain overall health and longevity.

The importance of support extends to various areas of life, including the workplace. Professional support, such as mentorship and collaboration, can enhance job satisfaction, performance, and career development. Mentors provide guidance, knowledge, and encouragement, helping individuals navigate their professional paths and achieve their career goals. Collaborative relationships with colleagues foster a sense of teamwork and mutual support, improving productivity and job satisfaction. Supportive work environments also promote mental health and well-being, reducing burnout and enhancing overall job performance.

In addition to personal and professional support, formal support systems, such as therapy and counseling, play a crucial role in mental health care. Professional therapists and counselors provide a safe and confidential space for individuals to explore their thoughts and feelings, develop coping strategies, and work through emotional and psychological issues. Therapeutic support can be particularly valuable for individuals dealing with mental health conditions, trauma, or significant life changes. It offers specialized guidance and interventions that promote healing and personal growth.

Support groups, whether for specific issues such as addiction, grief, or chronic illness, or for general emotional support, provide valuable opportunities for connection and shared experiences. In support groups, individuals can share their stories, gain insights from others who have faced similar challenges, and receive encouragement and understanding. These groups foster a sense of community and belonging, reducing feelings of isolation and providing a network of support.

Family support is another critical aspect of well-being. Healthy family relationships provide a foundation of emotional security and stability. Family members often share a deep understanding of each other's experiences and histories, offering unique insights and empathy. Supportive families encourage open communication, mutual respect, and shared problem-solving, helping individuals navigate life's ups and downs. However, it is important to recognize that not all family relationships are supportive. In cases where family dynamics are strained or unhealthy, seeking support from friends, professionals, or support groups can be crucial.

Friendships are also a vital source of support. Friends provide companionship, laughter, and shared experiences, enriching our lives and contributing to our happiness. They offer a listening ear, a shoulder to lean on, and a sense of camaraderie. Strong friendships are built on trust, mutual respect, and understanding, creating a safe space for individuals to be themselves. Friends can provide honest feedback, challenge us to grow, and celebrate our successes. These relationships enhance our emotional well-being and provide a sense of belonging.

In romantic relationships, support is essential for maintaining a healthy and fulfilling partnership. Supportive partners offer love, encouragement, and understanding, helping each other navigate the challenges of life. They communicate openly, resolve conflicts constructively, and provide emotional and practical assistance. A supportive romantic relationship fosters a sense of security and connection, enhancing both partners' well-being and happiness.

The importance of support is also evident in the context of parenting. Raising children is a demanding and often stressful responsibility, and having a network of support can make a significant difference. Supportive relationships with partners, family members, friends, and parenting groups can provide practical help, emotional encouragement, and shared experiences.

This support can reduce parental stress, increase confidence, and promote positive parenting practices. Children also benefit from a supportive environment, as it fosters their emotional and social development.

Support is not a one-way street; it involves both giving and receiving. Being a source of support for others can be deeply rewarding and fulfilling. It strengthens relationships, fosters a sense of purpose, and enhances our own well-being. Acts of kindness and support, whether big or small, create a positive ripple effect, contributing to a more compassionate and connected community. By offering support to others, we also reinforce our own social networks and build a sense of mutual trust and cooperation.

While support is crucial, it is important to recognize that not all relationships are supportive or healthy. Some relationships may be toxic, draining, or harmful to our well-being. It is essential to set boundaries and prioritize our own needs and health in these situations. This may involve limiting contact, seeking professional help, or ending the relationship if necessary. Prioritizing healthy, supportive relationships is key to maintaining our overall well-being.

Support can take many forms, and what constitutes effective support may vary from person to person. It is important to communicate our needs and preferences clearly to those around us. This helps ensure that we receive the type of support that is most helpful and meaningful to us. It is also important to be open to receiving support and to recognize that it is a sign of strength, not weakness, to seek help when needed.

In conclusion, the importance of support in our lives cannot be overstated. Supportive relationships provide emotional validation, practical assistance, encouragement, and a sense of belonging. They enhance our mental, emotional, and physical well-being, and help us navigate life's challenges with greater resilience and confidence. Support extends to various areas of life, including personal relationships, the workplace, and formal support systems such as therapy and support groups. By fostering and maintaining supportive connections, we can create a strong foundation for health, happiness, and personal growth. Both giving and receiving support enrich our lives and contribute to a more compassionate and connected community. Embracing the importance of support allows us to thrive and achieve our fullest potential.

ᵱᵱᵱ

"Seeking closure means coming to terms with our past and finding peace with it. It is the process of understanding and integrating our experiences. With closure, we free ourselves to embrace the future."

SIXTEEN

TRANSFORMING NEGATIVE PATTERNS

Transforming negative patterns is a crucial aspect of personal growth and emotional well-being. Negative patterns, whether they are habits, thought processes, or behaviors, can significantly hinder our ability to lead fulfilling and healthy lives. These patterns often develop over time, rooted in past experiences, learned behaviors, and deeply ingrained beliefs.

They can manifest in various forms, such as self-sabotage, chronic stress, relationship issues, or unhealthy coping mechanisms. The process of transforming these negative patterns involves self-awareness, commitment, and a willingness to change. By addressing and altering these patterns, we can create a more positive and empowered approach to life.

The first step in transforming negative patterns is self-awareness. This involves recognizing and understanding the patterns that are negatively impacting our lives. Self-awareness requires introspection and honesty, as it can be uncomfortable to confront our own behaviors and thoughts.

Reflecting on past experiences, identifying recurring issues, and acknowledging the consequences of these patterns are essential for understanding their origins and impact. Journaling, mindfulness, and talking with a trusted friend or therapist can help increase self-awareness and provide insights into our negative patterns.

Once we have identified the negative patterns, the next step is to understand their underlying causes. Negative patterns often stem from unresolved emotional issues, past traumas, or learned behaviors. For example, someone who grew up in a chaotic household might develop a pattern of avoiding conflict as a way to cope with stress.

Understanding the root causes of these patterns allows us to address them at their source rather than merely treating the symptoms. This deeper understanding can also foster compassion for ourselves, as we recognize that these patterns often developed as coping mechanisms in response to challenging circumstances.

Challenging and reframing negative thoughts is a crucial aspect of transforming negative patterns. Negative thought patterns, such as catastrophizing, overgeneralizing, or self-criticism, can reinforce harmful behaviors and beliefs. Cognitive-behavioral techniques can be particularly effective in addressing these thought patterns.

This involves identifying negative thoughts, examining the evidence for and against them, and replacing them with more balanced and constructive thoughts. For example, if someone has a pattern of thinking "I always fail," they can challenge this thought by recalling instances of success and reframing the thought to "I have had successes and failures, but I am capable of learning and improving."

Developing healthy coping mechanisms is essential for replacing negative patterns. Negative patterns often arise as ways to cope with stress, anxiety, or emotional pain. Finding healthier alternatives can help break the cycle of negative behavior.

This might include practicing mindfulness and relaxation techniques, engaging in physical activity, pursuing hobbies and interests, or seeking support from friends and professionals. By finding positive outlets for stress and emotions, we can reduce the reliance on negative patterns and promote overall well-being.

Setting realistic and achievable goals is another important step in transforming negative patterns. Goals provide direction and motivation, helping us focus on positive change. Breaking down larger goals into smaller, manageable steps can make the process less overwhelming and increase the likelihood of success. It is important to set goals that are specific, measurable, attainable, relevant, and time-bound (SMART). For example, if someone wants to improve their physical health, they might set a goal to exercise for 30 minutes three times a week, rather than an unrealistic goal of going to the gym every day.

Creating a supportive environment is crucial for sustaining positive changes. This involves surrounding ourselves with people who encourage and support our efforts to transform negative patterns. Friends, family, and support groups can provide valuable encouragement, accountability, and understanding. It is also important to create a physical environment that supports positive habits.

For example, if someone is trying to reduce their consumption of unhealthy foods, they might remove junk food from their home and stock up on healthy options instead.

Practicing self-compassion is essential throughout the process of transforming negative patterns. Change is challenging, and setbacks are a natural part of the journey. Being kind and understanding toward ourselves when we encounter difficulties helps maintain motivation and resilience.

Self-compassion involves recognizing that everyone makes mistakes and that growth is a gradual process. Rather than harshly criticizing ourselves for slip-ups, we can offer ourselves encouragement and support. This compassionate approach fosters a more positive and sustainable path to change.

Mindfulness is a powerful tool for transforming negative patterns. Mindfulness involves paying attention to the present moment with curiosity and non-judgment. It helps increase awareness of our thoughts, emotions, and behaviors, allowing us to observe them without becoming overwhelmed. Mindfulness practices, such as meditation, mindful breathing, and body scans, can help us develop greater self-awareness and emotional regulation. By practicing mindfulness, we can become more attuned to our negative patterns and create the space to respond to them with intention rather than reactivity.

Developing resilience is crucial for maintaining positive changes. Resilience is the ability to bounce back from adversity and continue moving forward despite challenges. Building resilience involves developing effective coping strategies, maintaining a positive outlook, and fostering supportive relationships. Practices such as gratitude, positive self-talk, and seeking out opportunities for growth and learning can enhance resilience. By building resilience, we can navigate the ups and downs of transforming negative patterns with greater ease and determination.

Seeking professional help can be an important part of the process. Therapists, counselors, and coaches can provide specialized guidance and support in addressing and transforming negative patterns. Therapeutic approaches such as cognitive-behavioral therapy (CBT), dialectical behavior therapy (DBT), and trauma-focused therapy can be particularly effective in helping individuals understand and change harmful behaviors and thought patterns.

Professional support can also provide a safe and confidential space to explore underlying issues and develop effective strategies for change.

Creating new, positive habits is essential for replacing negative patterns. Habits are formed through repetition and consistency, and developing new habits requires time and effort. Identifying positive behaviors that align with our goals and values and incorporating them into our daily routines can help establish new patterns. For example, if someone wants to develop a habit of regular exercise, they might schedule specific times for workouts, set reminders, and track their progress. Over time, these positive behaviors can become ingrained and replace negative patterns.

Reflecting on progress and celebrating successes is important for maintaining motivation and reinforcing positive changes. Taking time to acknowledge and appreciate the progress we have made, no matter how small, helps build confidence and momentum. Celebrating successes can involve rewarding ourselves with something enjoyable, sharing our achievements with others, or simply taking a moment to savor the accomplishment. This positive reinforcement helps to solidify new patterns and encourages continued growth.

Flexibility and adaptability are crucial for sustaining positive changes. Life is unpredictable, and the ability to adapt to changing circumstances is essential for maintaining progress. This involves being open to adjusting our goals and strategies as needed and being willing to try new approaches if something is not working. Flexibility allows us to navigate setbacks and challenges with greater resilience and to continue moving forward despite obstacles.

Transforming negative patterns is a continuous journey of self-discovery and growth. It requires patience, commitment, and a willingness to embrace change. By developing self-awareness, challenging negative thoughts, and cultivating positive habits and coping mechanisms, we can create a more empowering and fulfilling approach to life.

Support from others, self-compassion, mindfulness, and resilience are essential components of this process. Seeking professional help when needed and celebrating progress along the way can further enhance our ability to transform negative patterns and create lasting positive change. This journey ultimately leads to greater emotional well-being, healthier relationships, and a more fulfilling life.

"Building resilience involves developing effective coping strategies and maintaining a positive outlook. It is the strength to face life's challenges with determination. Through resilience, we thrive despite adversity."

SEVENTEEN
CULTIVATING GRATITUDE

Cultivating gratitude is a transformative practice that can significantly enhance our overall well-being and quality of life. Gratitude involves recognizing and appreciating the positive aspects of our lives, whether they are big or small. It shifts our focus from what we lack to what we have, fostering a sense of contentment and abundance. The practice of gratitude can have profound effects on our mental, emotional, and physical health, and it can improve our relationships and increase our resilience in the face of challenges. By consciously integrating gratitude into our daily lives, we can cultivate a more positive and fulfilling outlook.

Gratitude begins with awareness and mindfulness. It requires us to pay attention to the present moment and to notice the good things that are often overlooked. This can be as simple as appreciating a beautiful sunset, savoring a delicious meal, or acknowledging a kind gesture from a friend. By being mindful of these positive experiences, we can start to shift our focus from negative thoughts and complaints to a more appreciative mindset. This awareness helps to counteract the brain's natural tendency to focus on threats and problems, a phenomenon known as the negativity bias.

One of the most effective ways to cultivate gratitude is through the practice of keeping a gratitude journal. This involves regularly writing down things for which we are grateful. These can be significant events, such as a promotion at work, or small, everyday moments, such as a pleasant conversation or a cup of coffee. The act of writing helps to reinforce these positive experiences in our minds and makes us more aware of the good things in our lives. Over time, this practice can help to create a more grateful outlook, as we train our brains to focus on the positive.

Expressing gratitude to others is another powerful way to cultivate this practice. When we acknowledge and thank others for their kindness, support, or contributions, we not only make them feel appreciated but also reinforce our own sense of gratitude. This can strengthen our relationships and create a positive ripple effect, encouraging more acts of kindness and appreciation. Expressing gratitude can be done through verbal affirmations, written notes, or acts of kindness. The important thing is to be sincere and specific, expressing exactly what we are grateful for and why it matters to us.

Gratitude can also be cultivated through reflection and meditation. Taking a few moments each day to reflect on the things we are grateful for can help to deepen our appreciation. This can be done in a quiet, contemplative setting, where we can focus on our breath and bring to mind the people, experiences, and things that bring us joy and fulfillment. Guided gratitude meditations can also be helpful, as they provide structure and prompts to guide our thoughts. These practices can help to create a sense of calm and contentment, as we connect with the positive aspects of our lives.

Practicing gratitude does not mean ignoring or denying the challenges and difficulties we face. Instead, it involves acknowledging these difficulties while also recognizing the positive aspects of our lives. This balanced perspective can help us to navigate challenges with greater resilience and optimism. For example, during a difficult time at work, we might focus on the support of our colleagues or the learning opportunities that come with overcoming obstacles. By finding something to be grateful for, even in difficult situations, we can maintain a more positive outlook and reduce stress.

Gratitude can also be cultivated through acts of service and generosity. When we help others and contribute to our communities, we often feel a sense of fulfillment and purpose. These acts of kindness can remind us of the interconnectedness of all people and the importance of supporting one another. Volunteering, donating to charity, or simply helping a friend in need can foster a sense of gratitude for the opportunity to make a positive impact. This practice not only benefits others but also enhances our own sense of well-being and gratitude.

Another way to cultivate gratitude is by focusing on the present moment and savoring positive experiences. This involves fully engaging in and appreciating the good things that happen to us, rather than letting them pass by unnoticed. Savoring can be as simple as taking a moment to fully enjoy a delicious meal, relishing the warmth of the sun on our skin, or spending quality time with loved ones. By slowing down and savoring these moments, we can deepen our appreciation and create lasting memories of positive experiences.

Gratitude can also be fostered through the practice of gratitude rituals. These are regular practices or routines that help us to cultivate a sense of appreciation. For example, some people start or end their day by listing three things they are grateful for. Others might incorporate gratitude into their mealtime prayers or reflections. These rituals can help to make gratitude a consistent part of our daily lives, reinforcing the habit of looking for and appreciating the good things around us.

The benefits of cultivating gratitude extend beyond our mental and emotional well-being. Research has shown that gratitude can also have positive effects on our physical health. Grateful people tend to have lower levels of stress and depression, stronger immune systems, and better sleep. They are also more likely to engage in healthy behaviors, such as regular exercise and healthy eating. These physical benefits contribute to an overall sense of well-being and vitality, making gratitude a powerful tool for enhancing our quality of life.

Gratitude can also improve our relationships. When we express appreciation for others, we strengthen our connections and build trust and mutual respect. Grateful people are more likely to offer help and support to others, fostering a sense of community and cooperation. This positive dynamic creates a virtuous cycle, where acts of kindness and appreciation lead to stronger, more supportive relationships. By cultivating gratitude, we can create a more positive and harmonious social environment.

In addition to its personal benefits, gratitude can also have a broader impact on society. When people practice gratitude, they are more likely to engage in prosocial behaviors, such as volunteering, donating to charity, and helping others. These actions contribute to the well-being of the community and create a more compassionate and caring society. Gratitude can also promote a sense of collective responsibility and cooperation, encouraging people to work together for the common good. By fostering a culture of gratitude, we can create a more positive and supportive world for everyone.

Cultivating gratitude can be particularly important during times of difficulty and adversity. When we face challenges, it can be easy to focus on the negative and overlook the positive aspects of our lives. However, practicing gratitude during these times can help to build resilience and provide a source of strength and hope. By finding things to be grateful for, even in the midst of hardship, we can maintain a more balanced perspective and find the motivation to keep moving forward. Gratitude can act as a buffer against stress and anxiety, helping us to cope with difficult situations more effectively.

One of the key aspects of cultivating gratitude is consistency. Like any habit, gratitude requires regular practice to become ingrained in our daily lives. It is important to make gratitude a consistent part of our routine, whether through journaling, meditation, or simply taking a moment each day to reflect on what we are grateful for. By consistently practicing gratitude, we can train our minds to focus on the positive and develop a more appreciative mindset. This consistency helps to reinforce the habit of gratitude and makes it a natural and automatic part of our lives.

In conclusion, cultivating gratitude is a powerful and transformative practice that can significantly enhance our overall well-being and quality of life. By focusing on the positive aspects of our lives and expressing appreciation for the good things we have, we can shift our mindset from one of scarcity to one of abundance. Gratitude has profound effects on our mental, emotional, and physical health, and it can improve our relationships and increase our resilience in the face of challenges. Through practices such as journaling, expressing gratitude to others, meditation, and acts of service, we can integrate gratitude into our daily lives and create a more positive and fulfilling outlook. By consistently practicing gratitude, we can transform our lives and contribute to a more compassionate and supportive world.

"Living with purpose means aligning our actions with our deepest values and aspirations. It is the sense of direction that guides our decisions. By living purposefully, we create a life of meaning and fulfillment."

EIGHTEEN

LIVING AUTHENTICALLY

Living authentically is a journey toward understanding and embracing who we truly are. It means aligning our actions, decisions, and behaviors with our true selves, rather than conforming to external expectations or societal norms. Authenticity is about being genuine, transparent, and true to our values, beliefs, and passions. It involves self-discovery, self-acceptance, and the courage to live in accordance with our inner truth. Living authentically can lead to a more fulfilling and meaningful life, as it allows us to express our true selves and connect deeply with others.

The journey toward living authentically begins with self-awareness. This involves introspection and a willingness to explore our inner world. It requires us to ask ourselves deep and meaningful questions about who we are, what we value, and what we want from life. Self-awareness helps us identify our strengths, weaknesses, desires, and fears. By gaining a clearer understanding of ourselves, we can begin to make choices that reflect our true identity. This process of self-discovery is ongoing and evolves as we grow and change.

Self-acceptance is a crucial aspect of living authentically. It means embracing all parts of ourselves, including our imperfections and vulnerabilities. Self-acceptance involves recognizing that we are worthy of love and respect, just as we are. It requires letting go of the need for external validation and finding a sense of worth from within. This can be challenging in a society that often emphasizes perfection and conformity. However, self-acceptance allows us to live with greater confidence and peace, as we no longer feel the need to hide or change who we are to fit in.

Living authentically also involves aligning our actions with our values and beliefs. Our values are the guiding principles that shape our decisions and behaviors. They reflect what is most important to us and provide a sense of direction and purpose. When we live in accordance with our values, we experience a sense of integrity and fulfillment. This alignment requires us to make conscious choices that reflect our true selves, even when it is difficult or unpopular. It means standing up for what we believe in and staying true to our principles, even in the face of opposition.

Authenticity requires courage. It takes courage to be vulnerable and to show our true selves to the world. It means being honest about our feelings, thoughts, and experiences, even when they are difficult to share. Vulnerability is often seen as a weakness, but it is actually a sign of strength. It allows us to connect with others on a deeper level and to build genuine and meaningful relationships. By embracing vulnerability, we create an environment of trust and openness, where authenticity can flourish.

Living authentically also involves letting go of the need to please others. People-pleasing is a common behavior that stems from a desire for acceptance and approval. However, constantly seeking to please others can lead us to compromise our own needs and values. It can create a sense of resentment and disconnection from our true selves. By letting go of this need, we can focus on what truly matters to us and make decisions that reflect our own desires and aspirations. This does not mean being selfish or disregarding others' feelings, but rather finding a balance that allows us to honor our own needs while also being considerate of others.

Authenticity involves embracing our uniqueness and individuality. Each of us has a distinct set of qualities, experiences, and perspectives that make us who we are. Celebrating our uniqueness means recognizing and valuing what sets us apart from others. It means expressing our creativity, pursuing our passions, and sharing our gifts with the world. By embracing our individuality, we can live a more vibrant and fulfilling life, as we are no longer constrained by the need to conform to societal expectations.

Authenticity also requires us to be present and mindful. Being present means fully engaging in the moment and being aware of our thoughts, feelings, and actions. Mindfulness helps us stay connected to our true selves and make conscious choices that reflect our values. It allows us to respond to situations with clarity and intention, rather than reacting out of habit or external pressure. Mindfulness can be cultivated through practices such as meditation, deep breathing, and mindful movement. These practices help us develop greater self-awareness and create a sense of inner calm and balance.

Living authentically can have a positive impact on our relationships. When we are true to ourselves, we create deeper and more meaningful connections with others. Authenticity fosters trust, as people feel they can rely on us to be genuine and honest. It also allows us to attract people who resonate with our true selves, leading to more fulfilling and supportive relationships. By being authentic, we create an environment where others feel safe to be themselves, fostering mutual respect and understanding.

Authenticity can also enhance our professional lives. When we bring our true selves to our work, we are more likely to find meaning and satisfaction in what we do. Authenticity allows us to pursue careers that align with our passions and values, rather than settling for jobs that do not fulfill us. It also enables us to build genuine connections with colleagues and clients, fostering a positive and collaborative work environment. By being authentic in our professional lives, we can achieve greater success and fulfillment.

The journey toward living authentically is not without its challenges. It requires us to confront our fears and insecurities and to let go of old patterns and beliefs that no longer serve us. It involves making difficult decisions and taking risks. However, the rewards of living authentically are profound. It allows us to live with greater integrity, fulfillment, and joy. It enables us to build deeper and more meaningful relationships and to make a positive impact in the world.

One of the key challenges of living authentically is overcoming societal pressures and expectations. Society often imposes norms and standards that dictate how we should think, behave, and live. These pressures can make it difficult to stay true to ourselves, as we may fear judgment or rejection. It is important to recognize that living authentically may not always align with societal expectations, and that is okay. Authenticity involves finding the courage to be true to ourselves, even when it goes against the grain. It means trusting our own inner wisdom and following our own path.

Self-compassion is an essential aspect of living authentically. It involves being kind and understanding toward ourselves, especially when we face challenges or make mistakes. Self-compassion allows us to embrace our imperfections and vulnerabilities without judgment. It helps us stay connected to our true selves and maintain a sense of self-worth. By practicing self-compassion, we can navigate the ups and downs of life with greater resilience and grace.

Living authentically also involves setting boundaries. Boundaries protect our well-being and ensure that our needs and values are respected. They help us maintain a sense of balance and prevent us from being overwhelmed or taken advantage of. Setting boundaries requires us to be clear about our limits and to communicate them assertively. It involves saying no when necessary and prioritizing our own well-being. By setting and maintaining healthy boundaries, we create a safe and supportive environment for ourselves and others.

Personal growth and development are integral to living authentically. Authenticity is not a static state but a continuous journey of self-discovery and growth. It involves seeking out new experiences, learning from challenges, and evolving as individuals. Personal growth requires us to be open to change and willing to step out of our comfort zones. It involves cultivating a growth mindset, which is the belief that we can learn and grow through effort and experience. By embracing personal growth, we can continue to deepen our understanding of ourselves and live more authentically.

Living authentically can also have a positive impact on our mental and emotional well-being. When we are true to ourselves, we experience a greater sense of inner peace and contentment. Authenticity reduces the stress and anxiety that come from trying to meet external expectations or hide our true selves. It allows us to live with greater confidence and self-assurance. By being authentic, we create a sense of harmony between our inner and outer lives, leading to greater overall well-being.

In conclusion, living authentically is a journey of self-discovery, self-acceptance, and courage. It involves aligning our actions and decisions with our true selves, embracing our uniqueness, and letting go of the need to please others. Authenticity requires mindfulness, self-compassion, and the willingness to set boundaries. It can enhance our relationships, professional lives, and overall well-being. While the journey may be challenging, the rewards of living authentically are profound. It allows us to live with greater integrity, fulfillment, and joy, and to make a positive impact in the world. By embracing our true selves, we can create a more meaningful and authentic life.

"Self-awareness is the foundation of personal growth. It requires us to look inward and understand our thoughts, feelings, and behaviors. With self-awareness, we make conscious choices that reflect our true selves."

NINETEEN

THE JOURNEY OF SELF-DISCOVERY

The journey of self-discovery is a profound and deeply personal experience that involves exploring and understanding one's true self. It is a lifelong process of reflection, growth, and transformation, driven by a desire to live authentically and fully. This journey encompasses the exploration of our values, beliefs, passions, and purpose, as well as the recognition and acceptance of our strengths, weaknesses, and unique qualities. The path to self-discovery requires courage, openness, and a willingness to delve into the depths of our inner world. By embarking on this journey, we can gain a deeper understanding of who we are, what we want, and how we can live a more meaningful and fulfilling life.

Self-discovery begins with self-awareness. This involves turning our attention inward and becoming attuned to our thoughts, feelings, and behaviors. It requires us to be honest with ourselves and to examine our lives with curiosity and openness. Self-awareness helps us identify patterns, habits, and beliefs that shape our experiences and influence our actions. By paying attention to our inner world, we can begin to understand the motivations and desires that drive us, as well as the fears and insecurities that hold us back. This awareness is the foundation upon which self-discovery is built, as it allows us to see ourselves more clearly and to make conscious choices that align with our true selves.

One of the most important aspects of self-discovery is exploring our values. Our values are the guiding principles that define what is most important to us and influence our decisions and behaviors. They are the foundation of our sense of purpose and meaning. Understanding our values requires us to reflect on what we truly care about and what brings us fulfillment. This exploration can be facilitated by asking ourselves questions such as: What do I stand for? What do I want to contribute to the world? What brings me joy and satisfaction? By identifying our core values, we can make choices that are aligned with our true selves and live a life that is consistent with our deepest beliefs.

Another crucial aspect of self-discovery is understanding our beliefs and thought patterns. Our beliefs are the assumptions and interpretations we hold about ourselves, others, and the world. They shape our perceptions and influence our actions. Many of our beliefs are formed during childhood and are influenced by our upbringing, culture, and experiences. Some beliefs may be empowering and supportive, while others may be limiting and self-defeating. Self-discovery involves examining our beliefs with a critical and open mind, questioning their validity, and challenging those that no longer serve us. By transforming limiting beliefs into more empowering ones, we can create a more positive and expansive outlook on life.

Passions and interests are also key components of self-discovery. They are the activities and pursuits that ignite our enthusiasm and bring us joy. Exploring our passions involves experimenting with different activities, hobbies, and experiences to discover what resonates with us. It requires us to be open to new possibilities and to follow our curiosity. Our passions can provide valuable insights into our unique talents and abilities, as well as our sense of purpose.

By engaging in activities that we are passionate about, we can cultivate a sense of fulfillment and vitality, and express our true selves in meaningful ways.

The journey of self-discovery also involves recognizing and accepting our strengths and weaknesses. Our strengths are the qualities and abilities that come naturally to us and that we excel in. They are the areas where we can make our greatest contributions and achieve our highest potential. Our weaknesses, on the other hand, are the areas where we may struggle or feel inadequate. Recognizing our weaknesses requires humility and self-compassion. It involves acknowledging our imperfections without judgment and understanding that they are a natural part of being human. By accepting our strengths and weaknesses, we can develop a more balanced and realistic self-image, and leverage our strengths to overcome our challenges.

Self-discovery is also about understanding our emotions and developing emotional intelligence. Emotions are a fundamental part of our human experience, and they provide valuable information about our needs, desires, and boundaries. Developing emotional intelligence involves becoming aware of our emotions, understanding their underlying causes, and learning to manage them effectively. It requires us to be present with our feelings, to express them authentically, and to respond to them with compassion and understanding. By developing emotional intelligence, we can build healthier relationships, make more informed decisions, and navigate life's challenges with greater resilience.

The exploration of our purpose and meaning is another essential aspect of self-discovery. Our purpose is the sense of direction and intention that guides our actions and gives our life meaning. It is the answer to the question: Why am I here? Discovering our purpose involves reflecting on our values, passions, and experiences, and identifying the unique contributions we want to make to the world. It requires us to look beyond our own needs and desires and to consider how we can make a positive impact on others and the world around us. By living in alignment with our purpose, we can create a sense of fulfillment and satisfaction that transcends material success and external achievements.

The journey of self-discovery is not a linear process; it is filled with twists, turns, and unexpected detours. It requires patience, persistence, and a willingness to embrace uncertainty and change. There will be moments of clarity and insight, as well as periods of confusion and doubt. It is important to approach this journey with a sense of curiosity and openness, and to trust that each experience, whether positive or negative, is an opportunity for growth and learning.

One of the key challenges of self-discovery is overcoming the fear of judgment and rejection. The fear of being judged or rejected by others can prevent us from expressing our true selves and pursuing our passions. It can lead us to conform to societal expectations and to hide our authentic selves behind masks. Overcoming this fear requires courage and self-acceptance. It involves recognizing that our worth is not determined by others' opinions and that we have the right to be true to ourselves. By embracing our uniqueness and standing in our truth, we can build the confidence to live authentically and to create a life that is aligned with our deepest values and desires.

Self-discovery also involves letting go of the need for perfection. The pursuit of perfection can create a constant sense of inadequacy and dissatisfaction, as we strive to meet unrealistic standards. It can prevent us from taking risks, making mistakes, and learning from our experiences. Letting go of perfection involves embracing our imperfections and recognizing that they are a natural part of the human experience. It requires us to be kind and compassionate toward ourselves and to celebrate our progress and achievements, no matter how small. By letting go of perfection, we can create a more realistic and accepting self-image, and approach life with a sense of curiosity and openness.

Another important aspect of self-discovery is developing a sense of autonomy and independence. This involves taking responsibility for our own lives and making choices that reflect our true selves. It requires us to trust our own inner wisdom and to follow our own path, even when it diverges from the expectations of others. Developing autonomy involves setting boundaries, making decisions that align with our values, and taking ownership of our actions and their consequences. By cultivating a sense of autonomy, we can create a life that is true to ourselves and that reflects our unique identity.

The journey of self-discovery is also enriched by our relationships with others. Our interactions with others can provide valuable insights into ourselves and our behaviors. They can challenge us to grow, to see different perspectives, and to develop empathy and understanding. Building meaningful and authentic relationships requires us to be vulnerable, to communicate openly and honestly, and to show compassion and respect for others. By cultivating genuine connections, we can create a supportive and nurturing environment that fosters our self-discovery and personal growth.

In conclusion, the journey of self-discovery is a profound and transformative process that involves exploring and understanding our true selves. It requires self-awareness, self-acceptance, and the courage to live authentically. By examining our values, beliefs, passions, and purpose, and by recognizing and embracing our strengths and weaknesses, we can gain a deeper understanding of who we are and what we want from life. This journey involves developing emotional intelligence, overcoming fear and perfectionism, and cultivating autonomy and meaningful relationships. While the path of self-discovery may be challenging and filled with uncertainties, it ultimately leads to a more fulfilling and meaningful life, as we align our actions and decisions with our true selves and create a life that reflects our deepest values and desires.

ᐅᐅᐅ

"Mindfulness helps us stay connected to the present moment and our true selves. It is the practice of observing our experiences with openness and curiosity. Through mindfulness, we respond to life with greater clarity."

TWENTY

MOVING FORWARD WITH PURPOSE

Moving forward with purpose is a transformative journey that involves aligning our actions and decisions with our core values and deepest aspirations. Living with purpose means having a clear sense of direction and intention, knowing what truly matters to us, and making choices that reflect our true selves. It is about creating a life that is meaningful and fulfilling, one that resonates with our inner desires and contributes to the well-being of others. Moving forward with purpose requires self-awareness, commitment, and a willingness to embrace change and growth. By understanding and embracing our purpose, we can navigate life's challenges with greater resilience and confidence and create a positive impact on the world around us.

The journey to discovering our purpose begins with self-reflection and introspection. It involves asking ourselves deep and meaningful questions about who we are, what we value, and what we want to achieve in life. This process requires honesty and openness, as we delve into our passions, interests, and the experiences that have shaped us. Reflecting on our past achievements and challenges can provide valuable insights into our strengths, motivations, and the areas where we feel most fulfilled. By examining these aspects of ourselves, we can begin to identify the themes and patterns that point toward our purpose.

Understanding our core values is a crucial aspect of moving forward with purpose. Our values are the guiding principles that define what is most important to us and influence our decisions and behaviors. They provide a sense of direction and meaning, helping us prioritize our goals and actions. Identifying our core values requires us to reflect on what truly matters to us, what brings us joy and satisfaction, and what we want to contribute to the world. These values serve as a compass, guiding us toward a life that is aligned with our true selves and our aspirations.

Once we have a clearer understanding of our purpose and values, the next step is to set meaningful and achievable goals. Goals provide a roadmap for translating our purpose into actionable steps. They give us a sense of direction and motivation, helping us stay focused and committed to our path. It is important to set goals that are specific, measurable, attainable, relevant, and time-bound (SMART). This approach ensures that our goals are realistic and aligned with our purpose, making them more likely to be achieved. Breaking down larger goals into smaller, manageable steps can also make the process less overwhelming and increase our chances of success.

Taking action is a critical component of moving forward with purpose. It is not enough to simply have a sense of purpose and set goals; we must also take deliberate and consistent steps to achieve them. This requires discipline, perseverance, and a willingness to step out of our comfort zones. It involves making conscious choices that reflect our values and purpose, even when faced with challenges or setbacks. By taking action, we demonstrate our commitment to our purpose and create momentum toward achieving our goals.

Mindfulness and presence are essential for staying connected to our purpose. Being mindful means being fully engaged in the present moment, aware of our thoughts, feelings, and actions. It helps us stay focused on our goals and values, preventing us from becoming distracted by external pressures or fleeting desires. Mindfulness allows us to respond to situations with clarity and intention, rather than reacting out of habit or impulse. By cultivating mindfulness, we can stay grounded in our purpose and make decisions that are aligned with our true selves.

Resilience is another key factor in moving forward with purpose. Life is filled with challenges, obstacles, and uncertainties, and our ability to navigate these difficulties with resilience is crucial for maintaining our sense of purpose. Resilience involves developing effective coping strategies, maintaining a positive outlook, and staying committed to our goals despite setbacks. Practices such as gratitude, positive self-talk, and seeking support from others can enhance our resilience. By building resilience, we can face challenges with confidence and continue moving forward with purpose.

The importance of support and community cannot be overstated when it comes to moving forward with purpose. Surrounding ourselves with supportive and like-minded individuals can provide encouragement, accountability, and inspiration. Supportive relationships help us stay motivated and focused on our goals, and they offer valuable insights and feedback. Engaging with a community of people who share our values and aspirations can create a sense of belonging and connection, reinforcing our commitment to our purpose. It is important to seek out and nurture these relationships, as they play a vital role in our journey.

Flexibility and adaptability are also essential for moving forward with purpose. Our goals and circumstances may change over time, and it is important to remain open to new possibilities and to adjust our path as needed. Flexibility allows us to adapt to changing conditions and to stay aligned with our purpose, even when faced with unexpected challenges. It involves being willing to reassess our goals and strategies and to make adjustments that reflect our evolving understanding of ourselves and our purpose. By staying flexible and adaptable, we can navigate the twists and turns of life with greater ease and resilience.

Self-compassion is a crucial aspect of moving forward with purpose. Pursuing our purpose can be challenging, and we may encounter setbacks, failures, and moments of self-doubt. It is important to treat ourselves with kindness and understanding during these times, recognizing that growth and progress are not always linear. Self-compassion allows us to embrace our imperfections and to learn from our experiences without harsh self-judgment. By practicing self-compassion, we can maintain our motivation and resilience, and continue moving forward with a sense of inner strength and confidence.

Another important element of moving forward with purpose is continuous learning and growth. Living with purpose involves a commitment to personal and professional development. It requires us to seek out new experiences, acquire new knowledge and skills, and remain open to feedback and self-improvement. This mindset of lifelong learning helps us stay engaged and motivated, and it allows us to adapt to changing circumstances and to seize new opportunities. By embracing continuous learning and growth, we can stay aligned with our purpose and continue to evolve as individuals.

Gratitude is a powerful practice that can enhance our sense of purpose and fulfillment. By regularly reflecting on the positive aspects of our lives and expressing appreciation for what we have, we can cultivate a sense of contentment and abundance. Gratitude helps us stay focused on the present moment and recognize the progress we have made toward our goals. It also fosters a positive mindset, which can increase our resilience and motivation. Incorporating gratitude into our daily lives can reinforce our commitment to our purpose and enhance our overall well-being.

The journey of moving forward with purpose is deeply personal and unique to each individual. It requires us to listen to our inner voice, to trust our intuition, and to follow our own path. It involves making choices that reflect our true selves and our deepest values, even when it means going against the grain or facing uncertainty. By staying true to our purpose, we can create a life that is meaningful and fulfilling, one that resonates with our inner desires and contributes to the well-being of others.

In conclusion, moving forward with purpose is a transformative journey that involves aligning our actions and decisions with our core values and deepest aspirations. It requires self-reflection, self-awareness, and a commitment to personal growth. By setting meaningful goals, taking deliberate action, and staying mindful and resilient, we can navigate life's challenges with confidence and create a positive impact on the world around us. Support from others, flexibility, self-compassion, and continuous learning are essential components of this journey. By embracing our purpose and living authentically, we can create a life that is rich with meaning and fulfillment, and move forward with a sense of direction and intention.

ᐅᐅᐅ

"The journey of self-discovery is a lifelong process of reflection and transformation. It involves embracing our true selves and living authentically. In this journey, we find the path to a more fulfilling and meaningful life."

TWENTY-ONE
SUMMARY

The journey of self-discovery and personal growth is a transformative process that encompasses various aspects of our lives, from understanding and accepting ourselves to building resilience, seeking closure, and living authentically. Each step in this journey is crucial for achieving a fulfilling and meaningful life, as it involves aligning our actions and decisions with our core values and deepest aspirations. This summary encapsulates the essence of this journey, highlighting the importance of self-awareness, emotional intelligence, resilience, and purpose.

Self-discovery is the foundation of personal growth. It begins with self-awareness, which involves turning our attention inward and becoming attuned to our thoughts, feelings, and behaviors. Self-awareness requires honesty and openness, as we delve into our inner world to understand the motivations and desires that drive us, as well as the fears and insecurities that hold us back. This awareness is the foundation upon which self-discovery is built, allowing us to see ourselves more clearly and make conscious choices that align with our true selves.

Understanding our core values is a crucial aspect of self-discovery. Our values are the guiding principles that define what is most important to us and influence our decisions and behaviors.

Identifying our core values requires us to reflect on what truly matters to us, what brings us joy and satisfaction, and what we want to contribute to the world. These values serve as a compass, guiding us toward a life that is aligned with our true selves and our aspirations.

Exploring our beliefs and thought patterns is another essential aspect of self-discovery. Our beliefs shape our perceptions and influence our actions. Many of our beliefs are formed during childhood and are influenced by our upbringing, culture, and experiences. Some beliefs may be empowering and supportive, while others may be limiting and self-defeating. Self-discovery involves examining our beliefs with a critical and open mind, questioning their validity, and challenging those that no longer serve us. By transforming limiting beliefs into more empowering ones, we can create a more positive and expansive outlook on life.

Passions and interests are also key components of self-discovery. They are the activities and pursuits that ignite our enthusiasm and bring us joy. Exploring our passions involves experimenting with different activities, hobbies, and experiences to discover what resonates with us. It requires us to be open to new possibilities and to follow our curiosity. Our passions can provide valuable insights into our unique talents and abilities, as well as our sense of purpose. By engaging in activities that we are passionate about, we can cultivate a sense of fulfillment and vitality and express our true selves in meaningful ways.

Recognizing and accepting our strengths and weaknesses is also crucial for self-discovery. Our strengths are the qualities and abilities that come naturally to us and that we excel in. They are the areas where we can make our greatest contributions and achieve our highest potential. Our weaknesses, on the other hand, are the areas where we may struggle or feel inadequate. Recognizing our weaknesses requires humility and self-compassion. It involves acknowledging our imperfections without judgment and understanding that they are a natural part of being human. By accepting our strengths and weaknesses, we can develop a more balanced and realistic self-image and leverage our strengths to overcome our challenges.

Emotional intelligence plays a vital role in self-discovery and personal growth. Emotions are a fundamental part of our human experience, and they provide valuable information about our needs, desires, and boundaries. Developing emotional intelligence involves becoming aware of our emotions, understanding their underlying causes, and learning to manage them effectively. It requires us to be present with our feelings, to express them authentically, and to respond to them with compassion and understanding. By developing emotional intelligence, we can build healthier relationships, make more informed decisions, and navigate life's challenges with greater resilience.

The exploration of our purpose and meaning is another essential aspect of self-discovery. Our purpose is the sense of direction and intention that guides our actions and gives our life meaning. It is the answer to the question: Why am I here? Discovering our purpose involves reflecting on our values, passions, and experiences, and identifying the unique contributions we want to make to the world. It requires us to look beyond our own needs and desires and to consider how we can make a positive impact on others and the world around us. By living in alignment with our purpose, we can create a sense of fulfillment and satisfaction that transcends material success and external achievements.

Resilience is a key factor in personal growth and the ability to navigate life's challenges. Life is filled with obstacles and uncertainties, and our ability to bounce back from adversity is crucial for maintaining our sense of purpose. Resilience involves developing effective coping strategies, maintaining a positive outlook, and staying committed to our goals despite setbacks. Practices such as gratitude, positive self-talk, and seeking support from others can enhance our resilience. By building resilience, we can face challenges with confidence and continue moving forward with purpose.

Support and community play a vital role in our journey of self-discovery and personal growth. Surrounding ourselves with supportive and like-minded individuals can provide encouragement, accountability, and inspiration. Supportive relationships help us stay motivated and focused on our goals, and they offer valuable insights and feedback. Engaging with a community of people who share our values and aspirations can create a sense of belonging and connection, reinforcing our commitment to our purpose. It is important to seek out and nurture these relationships, as they play a vital role in our journey.

Flexibility and adaptability are essential for maintaining our sense of purpose and navigating the inevitable changes and challenges of life. Our goals and circumstances may change over time, and it is important to remain open to new possibilities and to adjust our path as needed. Flexibility allows us to adapt to changing conditions and to stay aligned with our purpose, even when faced with unexpected challenges. It involves being willing to reassess our goals and strategies and to make adjustments that reflect our evolving understanding of ourselves and our purpose. By staying flexible and adaptable, we can navigate the twists and turns of life with greater ease and resilience.

Self-compassion is a crucial aspect of personal growth and resilience. Pursuing our purpose can be challenging, and we may encounter setbacks, failures, and moments of self-doubt. It is important to treat ourselves with kindness and understanding during these times, recognizing that growth and progress are not always linear. Self-compassion allows us to embrace our imperfections and to learn from our experiences without harsh self-judgment. By practicing self-compassion, we can maintain our motivation and resilience, and continue moving forward with a sense of inner strength and confidence.

Continuous learning and growth are integral to living with purpose and achieving personal fulfillment. Living with purpose involves a commitment to personal and professional development. It requires us to seek out new experiences, acquire new knowledge and skills, and remain open to feedback and self-improvement. This mindset of lifelong learning helps us stay engaged and motivated, and it allows us to adapt to changing circumstances and to seize new opportunities. By embracing continuous learning and growth, we can stay aligned with our purpose and continue to evolve as individuals.

Gratitude is a powerful practice that can enhance our sense of purpose and fulfillment. By regularly reflecting on the positive aspects of our lives and expressing appreciation for what we have, we can cultivate a sense of contentment and abundance. Gratitude helps us stay focused on the present moment and recognize the progress we have made toward our goals. It also fosters a positive mindset, which can increase our resilience and motivation. Incorporating gratitude into our daily lives can reinforce our commitment to our purpose and enhance our overall well-being.

Living authentically is a central theme in the journey of self-discovery and personal growth. Authenticity involves being genuine, transparent, and true to our values, beliefs, and passions. It means aligning our actions and decisions with our true selves, rather than conforming to external expectations or societal norms. Authenticity requires courage, vulnerability, and self-acceptance. It allows us to express our true selves and connect deeply with others, creating more meaningful and fulfilling relationships. By living authentically, we can create a life that is rich with meaning and purpose.

The journey of self-discovery and personal growth is deeply personal and unique to each individual. It requires us to listen to our inner voice, trust our intuition, and follow our own path. It involves making choices that reflect our true selves and our deepest values, even when it means going against the grain or facing uncertainty. By staying true to our purpose and living authentically, we can create a life that is meaningful and fulfilling, one that resonates with our inner desires and contributes to the well-being of others.

In conclusion, the journey of self-discovery and personal growth is a transformative process that encompasses various aspects of our lives, from understanding and accepting ourselves to building resilience, seeking closure, and living authentically. Each step in this journey is crucial for achieving a fulfilling and meaningful life, as it involves aligning our actions and decisions with our core values and deepest aspirations. By embracing self-awareness, emotional intelligence, resilience, and purpose, we can navigate life's challenges with greater confidence and create a positive impact on the world around us. This journey ultimately leads to a richer, more fulfilling life, as we align our actions and decisions with our true selves and create a life that reflects our deepest values and desires.

Citation And References

This book represents the culmination of extensive research and meticulous analysis, incorporating a diverse range of sources, including numerous books, scholarly studies, and personal experiences. Additionally, I have scoured various websites to gather relevant information and data essential for the compilation of this work. I have taken every precaution to ensure the accuracy of the information presented and have diligently cited all sources to acknowledge their contributions.

Despite these efforts, the possibility of inadvertent errors remains. I deeply value the insights of my readers and appreciate any feedback that can help identify and rectify such inaccuracies. I encourage you to bring any discrepancies to my attention.

Your feedback is not only welcome but crucial, as it will aid in correcting current editions and enhancing the content of future ones. I am committed to maintaining the highest standards of accuracy and reliability in my work and thank you for your support and understanding.

Additionally, I firmly uphold the principle of freedom of speech and expression as guaranteed under Article 19(1)(a) of the Constitution of India, and I respect the diverse viewpoints and expressions of all readers.

ϷϷϷ

Other Books Of The Author

1. Empowering Minds: A Journey into Women's Self-Discovery and Power
2. The Dynamics of Motivation: Catalyzing Thought into Action
3. Meditation and Mental Well Being: The Path to Inner Peace and Clarity
4. The Psychology of Child Education: Nurturing Future Generations
5. Ethical Enlightenment: A Modern Guide to Living with Integrity
6. Voices of Empowerment: Stories of Women Rising Against Odds
7. Social Psychology in Everyday Life: Understanding Human Connections
8. The Essence of Motivational Speaking: Inspiring Change in Others
9. Balancing Acts: Women, Work, and the Will to Lead
10. Guiding with Grace: Raising Children with Compassion and Awareness
11. The Power of Positive Aging: Embracing Life After Fifty
12. Building Resilient Communities: Social Work in Action
13. The Ethical Educator: Principles for Teaching and Learning
14. From Insight to Impact: Social Psychology for a Better World
15. The Ethics of Empathy: A Guide to Ethical Living
16. The Science of Empowering the Self: Navigating Life's Challenges with Psychological Wisdom
17. The Mindful Conscious Leader: Meditation Techniques for Modern Management
18. Pioneering Spirit: Women's Pathways to Leadership and Empowerment
19. Feeling to Healing: The Role of Emotional Intelligence in Child Development
20. Transformative Talks and Words of Inspiration: Insights into Motivational Oratory

21. Green Ethics: A Path to Sustainable Living
22. Spiritual Integrity: Navigating Life with Moral Compassion
23. Clean Living, Clean Society: The Ethics of Cleanliness
24. Patriotic Spirits: Building a Nation on Positive Attitudes
25. Innovative Integrity & Vibrant Visions: The Ethical and Entrepreneurial Spirit of Gujarat
26. Youthful Visions, Endless Possibilities: Inspiring Ethics and Motivation in Children
27. Living Your Legacy: How to Motivate Others by Living Your Values
28. Secret of Healing Conversations: Ethical Practices in Counselling and Therapy
29. Creative Kindness: Crafting a Life of Compassion and Creativity
30. The Power of Appreciation: How Gratitude Can Transform Your Relationships
31. Bhagavad-Gita: Messages
32. Science of Art: The New Frontier of Fashion Modernism
33. Vivekananda's Virtues: A Blueprint for Modern Living
34. Empower Her: Navigating the Path to Women's Entrepreneurship
35. The Boundless Classroom: Innovations in Global Education
36. The Language of Leadership: Communicating with Authenticity and Impact
37. The Warrior's Mantra: Deciphering the Hanuman Chalisa
38. Echoes of Empathy: Transformative Stories of Social Service
39. Artful Living: Cultivating Creativity in Your Daily Routine
40. Finding Your Why: Discovering Your Passions and Charting Your Course
41. The Role of Social Media in Shaping Self-Esteem and Interpersonal Relationships among Adolescents
42. Karma's Tapestry: Weaving a Life of Selfless Service
43. Altruistic Alchemy: Transforming Lives Through Giving
44. The Blueprint of Pro-Activeness and Productivity: Crafting Habits for Success
45. The Simplicity with Grounded Wisdom: Embracing Authenticity

Bhajan

101. Pilgrimage of the Soul: Spiritual Journeys in India

❦❦❦

Contact

Dr. Minakshi Bansal
Social Activist
Ahmedabad, Gujarat, Bharat
minakshiindiag20@yahoo.com

❦❦❦

|| LOKAHA SAMASTHAHA SUKHINO BHAVANTU ||